TRADITIONAL IRISH LITERATURE
AND ITS BACKGROUNDS:
A BRIEF INTRODUCTION

TRADITIONAL IRISH LITERATURE AND ITS BACKGROUNDS: A BRIEF INTRODUCTION

A Revision of *The Shadow of the Three Queens*

George Brandon Saul

LEWISBURG
BUCKNELL UNIVERSITY PRESS

Associated University Presses, Inc.
Cranbury, New Jersey 08512

ISBN: 0-8387-7686-8

Printed in the United States of America

CONTENTS

PREFACE

In preparing this handbook, originally projected as a very concise aid to elementary students of Irish literature, I have merely sought, with a minimum of detail, to simplify by a sort of selective codification approach to a subject potentially of exciting interest to anyone sensitive to literature and its backgrounds, traditions, and associations. No other pretense is intended, and informed readers will be quick to weigh the large and miscellaneous indebtedness. Incidentally, translation of names generally follows the Rees brothers' *Celtic Heritage.*

General readers may discover that the information assembled here will be of aid in explaining historical and legendary implications present in much late- and post-Victorian Anglo-Irish literature, references to which are frequently given in footnotes. Meanwhile, I remain especially indebted to Professor Vernam Hull, whose generous reading of the original draft of my manuscript saved me from numerous errors of both accident and ignorance, though this acknowledgment is not to be construed as an effort to share blame for any undetected mistakes in the final version thereof or in the revised edition.

One other matter. In regard to the vexed question of the proper pronunciation of old Irish names, I would suggest that the reader may find convenient certain values of Alfred Nutt ("Cuchulainn, the Irish Achilles," *Popular Studies . . . ,* No. 8: London, 1900):

c:k; ch: as in Scotch *loch,* German *mich;* e:a, as in *fate,* or ai, as in *fair* (generally) ; u:oo, as in *look;* medial m *and* b: v when preceded *and* followed by e *or* i, but w when preceded or followed by a, o, *or* u.

It may be added that Ḟ = Ph and that accented vowels are long.

TRADITIONAL IRISH LITERATURE AND ITS BACKGROUNDS: A BRIEF INTRODUCTION

I. A NOTE ON LANGUAGE

Ancient, or *Continental, Celtic,* a branch—in the Western, or Centum, division—of the great Indo-European family of languages, was once spoken over much of central (and later also of western and southern) Europe. Out of it developed *Gallic (Gaulish),* the language of Gaul in Caesar's day—a language now almost unknown because of the extreme paucity of its remains, as well as two insular variants—*Goidelic (Gadhelic, Gaelic)* and *Brythonic (Britannic, British, Cymric).* From *Goidelic* came *Irish, Scotch Gaelic (Erse),* and *Manx*—the latter two sometimes regarded as offshoots of *Irish* proper; from *Brythonic* came (in somewhat marked divergence) *Welsh, Cornish,* and *Breton (Armoric).* Of these tongues, Irish, Welsh, Cornish, and Breton had each an ancient literature; and Irish, Scotch Gaelic, Manx, Welsh, and Breton were still being spoken in the twentieth century, though Cornish had all but died out as a spoken language during the eighteenth.[1]

Irish proper, with whose literature (the greatest among Celtic peoples) we shall be concerned, developed early (like English, an Indo-European cousin) an analytic tendency, with consequent changes in inflection, as well as changes in vocabulary and spelling. Historically viewed, its stages may be broadly indicated as follows :[2]

---

[1] On twentieth-century efforts at revival, *v.* J. J. Parry, "The Revival of Cornish . . . ," *PMLA,* LXI, 258 ff.

[2] Gerard Murphy—*Saga and Myth in Ancient Ireland* (Dublin, 1961), fn. 18, p. 14—prefers the following limits: "Old Irish, c. 600–c. 900; Middle Irish, c. 900–c. 1200; Early Modern Irish, c. 1200–c. 1650."

13

Old Irish: The Irish used from the seventh
or eighth century to about the
eleventh. Little material in Old
Irish is extant.

Middle Irish: Irish from the eleventh century to
the fifteenth.

Modern Irish: Irish since the fifteenth century.[3]

---

[3] Available 1968: D. Greene, *The Irish Language* (Cork, Mercier "Irish Life and Culture Series").

II. PREFIGURED IN HALF-LIGHT: A SHORT OUTLINE OF PRE-NORMAN IRISH HISTORY

Ancient tradition has claimed four occupations of Ireland after the tragedy of the Parthalonian settlement: by the Nemedians, harassed by the Fomorians and succeeded within about two centuries by the Firbolg; by the Tuatha Dé Danann ("Tribes of the Goddess Dana"); and by the Milesians, respectively.[1] Of these legendary races, the Nemedians are said to have been Greek Scythians. The Fomorians are pictured as one-armed, one-legged, gloomy sea-giants; the Firbolg, as a dark, small, undistinguished people; the Tuatha—of whom came the three queens Eire,[2] Fódhla, and Banba—as marvelous and half-divine masters of magic and sorcery; and the Milesians, as invaders from northern Spain whose coming the old annalists, imaginatively venturesome to an extreme limit of perhaps sixteen centuries, dated between 1700 and 800 B.C.

The Milesians are said to have been led by the sons of Miledh Easpáin ("Warrior of Spain," the name Latinized as "Milesius," but really an epithet for Golamh), of whom Eremon subsequently became ruler of northern, as Eber of southern, Ireland, or Ériu. In later times, after Christian ideas had got intertwined with pagan, attempts were

---

[1] Cf. IV, C, 1, *below*. Fomorian <*fo muirib:* "underseas."
[2] Or *Ériu*, whose Old Irish dative was *Érinn*.

15

made to link Irish with Biblical history and the ancestry of these Milesians was carried back through Gaelic and preceding Hebrew forebears straight to Adam, as evidenced by the account in the ninth-century *Historia Britonum* ascribed to Nennius.[3] Indeed, the complete fable includes Japhet among the thirteen Hebrew ancestors of Fenius Farsa, king of Scythia and founder of a school of languages, whose son Niul reputedly went to Egypt, married Scota (the Pharaoh's daughter), befriended Aaron, and had his own son—Gaedhal (whence "Gael")—healed of a serpent's bite by Moses! It was Golamh's grandfather, a remote descendant, who is said finally to have emigrated with four shiploads of his people from Gaethluighe to Spain. Incidentally, there is one story, as Eleanor Hull recalls in *Pagan Ireland* from the *Lebor Gabála Érenn* (see IV, C, 1, below), in which Cessair, a fictitious granddaughter of Noah, comes to Ireland forty days early to escape the Flood (in the year of the world 2242 according to the "Four Masters:" see *Annals of the Kingdom of Ireland,* ed. & trans. by J. O'Donovan: 7v.; Dublin, 2d edn., 1856), only to be drowned—on the authority of a later tale—with her brother and fifty maidens, though her husband, Fintan, escapes, to appear in the sixth century as a man over five thousand years old!

Modern scholarship, of course, suggests less diverting, though unhappily also less assured, ideas and speculations concerning the remote history of Ireland and its successive occupants. Whatever may be hazarded as to their predecessors (? Cruithin, Firbolg: O'Rahilly's Belgae, Laginians), it appears at present reasonable to postulate a remote Central-European background for the

---

[3] Cf. *The Irish Version of the Historia Britonum of Nennius,* ed. and trans. J. H. Todd (Dublin, 1848).

last conquerors of pre-Christian days, presumably Gaelic, or "Q-speaking," Celts (Goidels). These invaders—cousins to their predecessors, the British, or "P-speaking," Celts (Brythons)—seemingly entered Ireland from Gaul during the first century B.C. Pictured as a tall, fair people with "red-blond" hair who spoke a language somewhat closely related to Latin (cf. L. *libri*—Ir. *leabhair* or *leabhra, literae—litreacha,* etc.), they were originally labeled *Hiberni,* but later *Scotti* ("raiders"), by the Romans. They are said to have named their island "Ériu."

However cloudy their antecedents, these conquerors appear to have merged culturally with the conquered and to have developed into monarchists who divided the island into kingdoms known as "fifths": Ulster (*Uladh,* with Emain its legal capital), Leinster (*Laigin,* its capital Dinn Ríg), Connacht (*Connachta,* its capital Cruachan), Meath (*Mide,*[4] its capital Tara[5]), and Munster (*Mumu,* its capital Temuir Erann). Eastern Munster came later to be known as "Ormond" (*Urmumu*), Southern Munster as "Desmond" (*Desmumu*)[6]; and by the beginning of the eleventh century, the fifths had been subdivided into approximately a hundred small states, known as *tuatha.*

Among these early Irish, traditional concerns like law and literature appear to have been in the hands of the *filid* (poets and seers), a body persisting beyond the time of the Anglo-Norman invasion; religion, similarly, was presumably in charge of the druids, though one can speak

---

[4] Named for Nemed's head druid.
[5] Which in the view of Alwyn and Brinley Rees (*Celtic Heritage,* London, 1961, p. 163) "originally symbolized the cosmos of the gods as opposed to the chaos of the demons." It was supposedly named (*Temair*) from Eremon's queen, Tea.
[6] Actually, the early references generally speak of Ulster, Leinster, Connacht, and "the two Munsters" (East and West). The Rees brothers (*ibid.,* 119) assert neither tradition "more authentic than the other."

with less certainty here. Remote Irish literature, of course, was orally preserved and transmitted; there is no convincing evidence of writing antedating the fourth or fifth century of the Christian era—*i.e.,* prior to the infiltration of Latin culture. Even the antiquity of *ogam*—a species of alphabetic engraving on stone or wood—is suspect, inception of the symbols (all but universally regarded as adaptations from the Latin alphabet, though derivation from a Greek alphabet of the fifth and sixth centuries B.C. has also been proposed) being now generally assigned to a time shortly after the introduction of Christianity,[7] though Dillon (*Early Irish Society,* Dublin, 1954, p. 10) has speculated on the fourth century.

What is sometimes called "sober history" can speak with only hesitant assurance about many facets of Irish tradition antedating the eleventh century, though its romance-drunken substitute, the fabric of poets and annalists, talks freely—and colorfully. Nevertheless, scholars like Dillon and Hyde (who bases his position on both linguistic and other scientific evidence—such as accurate dating of the appearance of comets) are inclined to place considerable credence in the historical pretensions of many of the old accounts. So there may be the common truth of fact as well as the uncommon truth of imagination in recounting the Gaelic crushing by Tuathal of a "Firbolg" revolt led by Cairbre Cinn Cait about A.D. 100, prior to the union of Meath and Connacht. It was reputedly Tuathal's descendant "Conn of the Hundred Battles" (*Conn Cédcathach*) who, a century later, established the central monarchy but eventually divided Ireland with his southern

---

[7] One may cf. J. Vendryes, "L'écriture ogamique et ses origines," *Études Celtiques,* IV, 83–116; and L. Gerschel, "Origine et premier usage des caractères ogamiques," *Ogam,* IX, 151–73. Between three and four hundred *ogam* inscriptions are extant, but not only in Ireland.

rival, Eoghan Mór ("Mogh Nuadat": "Servant of Nuada"), the line separating "Conn's Half" from "Mogh's Half" running along the Escir Riada, a stretch of sandhills between Dublin and Galway.

It is Conn who is counted head of the line of "high kings" persisting beyond Clontarf; it was "Conn's Race" expanded their Connacht-Meath kingdom by adding territory from Ulster and Leinster, while the Eoghanacht in turn built up a great Munster kingdom. Conn's grandson, Cormac Mac Airt, who flourished during the third century, has particular distinction in being remembered not merely as the founder of Tara[8] as the High King's capital and as the builder of the "five great roads" converging in that center, but as the reputed organizer of the *Fianna,* a military force which entered heroic legend.

The High King (*ard-rí Éireann*), it should be understood, held subject to himself the kings of the fifths, who were in turn overlords to the kings of those hegemonies known as "great *tuaths.*" The lowest order of kingship was that of *rí* (Lat. *rēx,* Skr. *rājā*), king of a *tuath* (a state of perhaps 25,000 population)—really an elected military leader and assembly-president whose allegiance was to a *rí mór-tuath.* Qualifications for a kingship included, in Dr. Record's neat summary,[9] "physical perfection, ability in feats of arms, daring in warfare and cattle-raiding, generosity, nobility, erudition, and a keen sense of justice." Incidentally, an assembly could depose an unsatisfactory king, and kingship was not originally hereditary.

Next to the king among the primitive Irish ranked the

---

[8] Cf. R. A. S. Macalister, *Tara* . . . (London, 1931).
[9] M. T. Record, *A Sociological Study of Ancient Irish Culture* (Ph.D. diss., Yale University, 1938), 281–82.

tanist (one recalls James Stephens' "Kings and Tanists," in *Kings and the Moon*)—a designated royal successor, generally that near relative of the king supposed to possess the greatest capability for rule. The tanist, however, rarely came to the throne, since given kings were likely either to die in battle or to be murdered, their thrones in any case susceptible to usurpation, and even in peaceful times elections—following a process of divination managed by the druids—were prescribed. In Eleanor Hull's description,[10] "A white bull was killed, and a man ate of his flesh and drank from the broth. He was then put into a magic sleep by the incantation of the Druids; and he was supposed to see in a dream the person who was to be made king; out of his sleep he gave a description of the person whom he saw, who was then elected by the people." (The High King had to stand on the *Lia Fail*, or "Stone of Destiny," reputedly brought by the Tuatha Dé Danann and possessed of a roar to acclaim rightful sovereignty standing upon it. This stone—in one tradition a "stone penis"—is commonly, though not universally, believed to be beneath the British coronation throne in Westminster Abbey, as having been supposedly carried into Scotland by fifth-century Irish raiders and taken from Scone into England by Edward I. Some hold, however, that it is identifiable with a stone preserved upright on the Hill of Tara.)

A given king held the largely theoretical allegiance of sub-kings or nobles through hostages—unfortunately not exempt from torture, however well-born themselves; periodically he made "free circuits" about the country,

---

[10] *Pagan Ireland* ("Epochs of Irish History—I": Dublin, 1923), 43–44. Cf. E. S. Hartland, "The Voice of the Stone of Destiny," *Folklore Jour.,* XIV, 1 (Mar. 1903), and see *The Destruction of Da Derga's Hostel.*

a heavy burden to his hosts (cp. the British royal "prog-
resses"). He had to lead the army, preside over assemblies, and control relations with other kings. It is said that
in early days his normal calendar designated Sunday for
feasting, Monday for government, Tuesday for chess,
Wednesday for greyhound-coursing, Thursday for home
life, Friday for horse-racing, and Saturday for legal arbi-
tration. Incidentally, it has been suggested[11] that the early
Celts, like various other Indo-Europeans, were probably
"ruled by priestly kings," this circumstance explaining the
eventual ascription to Irish kings of certain aspects of
divinity and accounting for the belief (shared by the early
Welsh) "that there would be bad crops as a punishment
for bad rulers."

It may be next observed, by way of resuming a chrono-
logical view, that Niall of the Nine Hostages[12] (from
whom descended the ruling race of "Ui Néills" which persisted to 1022) reigned in Tara from 380 to 405; and
that the fifth century saw both Irish invasions of Britain
and the founding (in 470) of Argyle (the kingdom of
"the eastern Gael") by the Antrim prince Fergus Mac
Erc and his brothers.

The same century witnessed, in 432, if the traditional
claim be accepted, the coming of St. Patrick (Patricius
Magonus Sucatus), who—a Roman decurion's son from
Bannaventa, Britain—had at seventeen reputedly been
carried by raiders into slavery in Ireland, subsequently
to escape to Gaul, study at Auxerre, and return as a missionary apparently faced by little real opposition except

---

11 J. Pokorny, "Origin of Druidism," *Celtic Rev.*, V, 1–20.—Cf. J. Rhys,
Lectures on . . . Religion . . . (London, 1888; 2d ed., 1892), 308; and
Celtic Britain (London and New York, 1882; 3d ed., London, 1904), 64.
12 On the epithet, see T. F. O'Rahilly, *Early Irish History and Mythology*
(Dublin, 1946), 233.

from the druids and *filid*. Christianity, of course, had reached Ireland from Gaul before his advent (O'Rahilly, *The Two Patricks:* Dublin, 1942, postulates an earlier "Patrick"—Palladius Patricius—sent as first Christian bishop in 431, about three decades before the better-known Patrick, with whom he became confused, arrived).[13] But "Patrick the Briton," according to tradition, proved (assisted within a few years by Secundinus, Auxilius, and Iserninus) to be the most vital agent, his activities radiating from his center (established in 443) at Armagh, Ulster, and himself dying in 461 (about thirty years earlier than O'Rahilly concedes). By 490 Oengus of Munster had emerged as the first Christian king, and the Christians must be thanked for bringing learning, education, and new crafts, as well as religion, to the island; certain abbeys became notable centers of Latin culture (the first of them Clonard, Meath, organized *c.* 540 by the abbot-bishop St. Finnian), and presently (? seventh century) Irish began to be written in the Latin alphabet. (Incidentally, Greek and Hebrew were taught as well as Latin.) Within the ecclesiastical organization itself—though a monastic system, with many bishoprics, prevailed—local conditions led to the magnifying of the importance of abbots, whose succession was apt to be an hereditary affair; further, the Irish church, segregated from the Mother Church by Teutonic movements in Britain and Europe, though continuing allegiance to Rome, developed certain rites and practices of its own.

The sixth century, which saw the initiation of three centuries of considerable sea intercourse with southern Gaul,

---

[13] Cp. *Irish Ecclesiastical Record,* Mar. 1953.—Palladius' mission is dated in the *Annals of Ulster.*—See also R. P. C. Hanson, *Saint Patrick . . .* (Oxford, 1968).

revealed much missionary activity, largely stimulated by that of Columba (or Colum Cille: "the Dove of the Church") in Britain. This man, by birth a prince of Niall's house, had founded his mission at Iona in 563; he died in 597—the year in which Augustine came to Kent. Indeed, the period from 600 to 800 is particularly notable in the history of the Irish church (despite that church's differences with Rome over the dating of Easter and the matter of tonsures); and many Irish monks, priests, and scholars of the time became famous on the Continent as churchmen, teachers, and scribes.

By 800 there was a strong cultural unity in Ireland, but unfortunately much political subdivision, with the High King little more than a figurehead—a condition highly favorable to the Norse invaders who, under Thorgest, made their initial attempt to establish a kingdom in the island in 831. Thorgest was captured and drowned by Malachy, King of Meath, in 845, but further invasion followed—with ultimate intermarriage of "Gael and Gall" and some respite in the fighting.

In 914 came a more determined Norse invasion, led by Ragnall and Sitric. Within two years Dublin had been occupied: at the time it was, like the other Irish seaports, since the country contained nothing worthy of being called a town, merely a collection of huts, with a wooden bridge over the Liffey (though bridges also appear to have been almost unknown in early times). Then Niall Black-knee, the High King, fought Sitric at a ford on the Liffey, only to be slain, his forces defeated. In 920 the Norse occupied Limerick, thus completing a series of viking entrenchments scattered south- and southwest-ward along the coast line from Dublin, where a Norse line of kings was seated. Munster was subjugated, and when Olaf of the Sandals defeated the Irish High King, Domnall, in 977, Meath also fell under oppression.

Norse domination was finally ended by Malachy, King of Meath, and Brian Boru, a prince of Thomond. Details of battle, parley, and further battle are very complicated —and rendered none the less so by the loves and machinations of Gormflaith,[14] to whom Brian became third husband. The latter eventually emerged as High King, Malachy yielding claim in 1002; thereafter the two co-operated to revive Ireland's riddled culture, rebuilding churches, schools, and monasteries, and in general trying to restore in some degree what the Norse marauders had destroyed. But Gormflaith—unable to forgive her second husband, Malachy (who had conquered her first, the Norseman Olaf), for repudiating her—stirred up her brother of Leinster and her son of Dublin against this northern regent of Brian's: the two rebels, in responding, called in Norse aid; and on Palm Sunday, 1014, the aged Brian (himself no longer able to fight) joined Malachy and their allies for the battle of Clontarf, which proved a decisive victory for them and their Irish, though the unguarded Brian was slain in his tent by a fleeing Norseman.[15] Thereupon Malachy became High King, the Ui Néill dynasty ending with his death in 1022. The conquered Norse meanwhile settled down, mingled with their conquerors, and became Christians, their coastal towns developing into trading centers and their mother tongue contributing very slightly to the vocabulary of Irish.

After Malachy's death there ensued a long period of internal squabbling and usurpation among various princes which weakened for the Norman invasion the land temporarily unified under Brian. The period following the final

---

[14] The heroine of the present writer's novella *The Wild Queen* (1967).
[15] Cf. Lady Gregory's *Kincora*.

defeat of the Norse, however, saw increased interest in the recording of Irish history—which led to some absurdities. According to Mac Neill,[16] "The Irish historians found in Latin histories a set of definite epochs by which antiquity was divided: the beginning of the Assyrian Empire, the beginning of the Persian Empire, the usurpation of the Magi in Persia, and the beginning of Alexander's empire. The chronology of the Irish invasions was settled by the easy process of making each invasion coincide exactly in time with each of these epochs."

When the effects of the Continental renaissance of the eleventh and twelfth centuries began to be felt in Ireland, the need for Church reform started to be re-stressed. As Curtis puts it,[17] "Ireland was asked to accept all the essentials of the Western Church, the supreme authority of Rome, conformity to one ritual, canonical marriage, a proper episcopate under Roman authority, celibacy and tithes for the clergy, and the freedom of the Church from lay domination." After years of hesitation, the Irish Church really did yield to the desires of Rome and the new order was organized under four archbishops. But political conditions remained bad, and when the High King Turloch O'Connor died in 1156, Murcertach Mac Lochlann pushed aside his son, winning the office for himself in 1162. However, Murcertach's brutal blinding of a vassal king led to his own slaying in a consequent revolt and to Rory O'Connor's succession. Petty fighting among princelings presently led a certain Dermot Mac Murrough[18] to go to Bristol in search of English support, which he obtained—partly by making a match between

---

16 E. Mac Neill, *Celtic Ireland* (Dublin and London, 1921), 27–28.—As quoted by Record.
17 E. Curtis, *A History of Ireland* (London, 1936—and later), 38.
18 Cf. Standish James O'Grady, *The Departure of Dermot* (Dublin, 1917); W. B. Yeats, *The Dreaming of the Bones.*

his attractive daughter Eva and Richard, Earl of Pembroke. Supported thus by the Normans (who had already conquered the Welsh), this former King of Leinster returned to Ireland in 1167. Four years later he died and Richard ("Strongbow") became King of Leinster. Aided by lieutenants like Maurice Fitzgerald (hence the "Geraldines"), he was essentially master of Ireland the same year, in October of which Henry II of England himself arrived with an army, reputedly commissioned—though the authenticity of the apparently lost bull has been questioned—by Pope Adrian IV. The Irish kings and chiefs submitted, as did the clergy—the latter with the result that final reforms in line with Roman doctrine were achieved. But Henry promptly proved himself a double-dealer, appointed Hugh de Lacy his viceroy, and organized matters on a feudal basis, with doors opened wide to exploitation. Recalled to England in April of 1172 to meet the situation resulting from Becket's murder, Henry made his peace with the new pope, Alexander III, who, in Curtis' phrase,[19] "conferred" on him "dominion over the Irish people." Curtis adds flatly,[20] "Later generations of Irishmen right up to the seventeenth century fully accepted the papal donation as a fact—witness the Remonstrance of the Irish chiefs to the Pope in 1317—but both then and later they accused the crown of England of having violated the rights of the Irish Church and the Irish people." At any rate, it is fairly clear that native Irish authority in both church and state had pretty well disintegrated by the end of the twelfth century.

---

[19] Curtis, 56.
[20] *Ibid.*, 57.

III. WEIGHTS AND BALANCES: SOCIOLOGICAL CONSIDERATIONS OF PARTICULAR INTEREST

A. Ancient Religion and Associated Mythology[1]

The religion of the ancient Irish is largely a matter of speculation—and consequently, of dispute. For instance, Douglas Hyde's belief[2] that "the pagan Irish once possessed a large pantheon, probably as highly organized as that of the Scandinavians" is sharply opposed by Record's conclusion[3] that the Irish had "no pantheon of deities, no organized system of worship, no regularly constituted priesthood": that theirs "was merely a body of rather crude animistic belief, a group of practices evolved to deal with the forces postulated by that belief, and a number of

---

[1] For extensive discussion, cf. especially H. d'A. de Jubainville, "Le Cycle Mythologique Irlandais et la Mythologie Celtique," *Cours de Littérature Celtique,* II (Paris, 1884. Trans. by R. I. Best, *The Irish Mythological Cycle and Celtic Mythology,* Dublin, 1903) ; G. Murphy, *Saga and Myth in Ancient Ireland* (Dublin, 1961) ; A. Nutt, "Essay upon the Irish Vision of the Happy Otherworld and the Celtic Doctrine of Rebirth," in Meyer-Nutt edn. of *The Voyage of Bran* (2 vols.: London, 1895–97) ; T. F. O'Rahilly, *Early Irish History and Mythology* (Dublin, 1946) ; M. T. Record, *A Sociological Study of Ancient Irish Culture* (Yale diss., 1938) ; Alwyn and Brinley Rees, *Celtic Heritage* (London, 1961) ; T. W. Rolleston, *Myths and Legends of the Celtic Race* (Rev. edn., New York, 1913) ; Marie-Louise Sjoestedt, *Dieux et héros celtiques* (Paris, 1940. Trans. by M. Dillon, *Gods and Heroes of the Celts,* London, 1949) ; A. G. van Hamel, "Aspects of Celtic Mythology," *Procs. of the Brit. Acad.,* XX (1934) ; J. Vendryes, "La religion des Celtes," *Les religions de l'Europe Ancienne* (Paris, 1948).
[2] *A Literary History of Ireland* (London, 1899), 55.
[3] *Op. cit.,* Fn. 1, 299.

human agents who acted as intermediaries between those forces and the men of the earth."

Certainly there appears, for one thing, to be no really convincing evidence arguing a belief in, as distinguished from speculation about, life after death,[4] despite the concept of a "Land of the Young" (or ". . . of Promise," or ". . . of Fair Women")—located sometimes in a mound, but usually either on an island to the northwest of Ireland or at the bottom of a lake—to which mortals could be transported. This concept is in some degree related to further belief in *side* ("shee")—inhabitants of burial tumuli (though the term is also applied to the mounds themselves), conceived of as immortal and, usually, invisible, though capable of various types of intercourse—including that of marriage—with humans. The male of this folk was known as a *fer-síde;* the female, as a *ben-síde* (modern "banshee")—eventually conceived of as a spirit attendant on given families who could be heard keening at night when prophecy of the approaching death of some family member was her mission. (Incidentally, *ben-síde* lovers of mortals were known as *lennan-síde.*) In the Fenian cycle of tales the *side* appear identifiable with the Tuatha Dé Danann (pictured in the Mythological Cycle as driven underground after their defeat by the Milesians at Taillte, County Meath)—a folk suggestive in character of both the human and the divine, and a folk whose leaders have been said to be buried in the hillock-like tombs on the Boyne nigh Drogheda. The *side* are generally thought of as living (and fighting!) like mortals, though in greater than mortal magnificence, in their numerous mounds or "fairy palaces," of which the most fearsome was probably the cave of Cruachan, in

---

4 Cf. Rees, Fn. 1, 324–25.

Connacht, known as the "Hell-gate of Ireland" because of its goblins and monstrous, livid birds, whose very breath was poison. On Samhain eve (Halloween), the doors between the world of the *síde* and that of mortals were believed open, with ingress and egress reciprocally possible.

As Eleanor Hull long since admitted,[5] most of the older Irish gods and goddesses are now mere names, known by casual reference and through certain place names, but honored by practically no extant romances concerning them, while even "the romances connected with the younger gods are rare." (Whether, incidentally, there was among the Irish any worshipping of idols, with offering of human sacrifices, seems to be another open question —unless Patrick Joyce was correct in attributing ascriptions of such practice to the imagination of Christian scribes.) Worshipped or unworshipped, the divinities most likely to find literary mention may be briefly identified as follows:

> *Ana* (otherwise *Anu, Dana, Danu,* or *Danann*—whence "Tuatha Dé Danann": "The tribes, or peoples, of the Goddess Dana") : a beneficent goddess (sometimes regarded as the mother of the Dé Danann divinities as a family) ; mother of *Brian, Iuchar,* and *Iucharba*—of confused history, but so well nursed by Ana that she was regarded in Munster as the goddess of plenty and the two conical mountains near Killarney came to be called "The Paps of Dana."
>
> *Bel* (*Bil, Bial*) : a mysterious god, associated with the "Beltine Fires" between which it has been supposed the druids drove cattle at the opening of the summer season ("Beltine"[6]) to

---

[5] *A Text-Book of Irish Literature* (2 vols.: Dublin & London, 1906–08), I, 7.
[6] The pagan Irish observed the following calendar of seasonal openings: *Oimelc* ("the first milk of the sheep": Hull, *Pagan Ireland,* 87)—1 Feb., the start of spring, later St. Brigid's Day; *Beltine*—1 May; *Lughnasadh* (with reference to the games of Lugh)—1 Aug., the start of autumn, later "Lammas"; *Samhain*—1 Nov., the beginning of winter, later "Allhallows Day."—Cf. J. G. Frazer, *Golden Bough:* New York, 1-vol. edn., 1930; 617

prevent disease during the rest of the year. Eleanor Hull thinks St. Patrick was perhaps responsible for transferring the lighting of these great fires to "Midsummer day, or St. John's Eve."[7]

Buanann: another beneficent goddess, who reared (and taught arms to) heroes.

Cian: son of Diancecht: father of *Lugh* by *Ethlenn*—the latter apparently the daughter of Balor by Cian's own wife; murdered by the sons of Tuireann.

Credne: brother of Diancecht; a brazier.

The Dagda (or *Dagda Mor*: "the good god," though *Dagda* has also been translated "good hand"): a wise and kindly god who supposedly ruled Ireland for eighty years and whose wife is variously named "Lie," "Guile," or "Disgrace"! He is pictured in *The Second Battle of Moytura* as grotesquely fat and hardly able to walk, with a club so heavy it required eight men to draw it on a wheeled car, a ladle large enough to hold a man and a woman, and a harp musically responsive only to his call. He had three daughters, all named *Brigid,* goddesses respectively of poetry, smithwork, and medicine; and two sons—*Bodb Derg* (father of the goddess *Bugh*) and *Aengus (Oengus) Mac-in-Og* (the younger son), magician, god of love and beauty, and special favorer of Diarmuid and Grainne: sometimes called "Aengus na Brugh" because his foster-father, Elcmar, had a *brugh* (mansion) on the Boyne until tricked out of it by Manannan.[8]

Diancecht: physician and god of medicine.

Donn: "god of the dead," in Greene's phrase.

Etan: daughter of Diancecht; a poet.

Goibniu: brother of Diancecht; originally a smith, but later an architect known as "the Gobhan Saer."[9]

Ler: god of ocean; well known also as the Welsh *Llyr,* father

---

ff.—See also E. Knott, "Hallowe'en, or Samhain in Ancient Ireland," *Irish Packet,* V, 110 (4 Nov. 1905). 123.

[7] *Op. cit.,* Fn. 6, 88.

[8] This *brugh* is generally identified with modern New Grange, north of the river. On this prehistoric marvel, see the fascinating *New Grange and the Bend of the Boyne,* by Sean P. Ó Ríordáin and Glyn Daniel (London: Thames and Hudson, 1964).

[9] See Ella Young's *The Wonder-Smith and His Son* and cf. her "Adventures of the Gabbaun Saor and His Son," serially published in the *Dublin Magazine,* I (1923–24), with installments beginning on pp. 41, 121, 205, 317, 430, and 513; also Yeats's *The Grey Rock.*

of Branwen (who married an Irish king) and Bran (hero of voyage tales).

Luchtině: brother of Diancecht; a carpenter.

Lug(h) (Welsh *Llew*; cp. "Leyden," "Lyons," "Laon") : young god of "light and knowledge," radiant like the sun; said to have attained full growth in infancy and to have led the Tuatha Dé against the Fomorians under "Balor of the Evil Eye" in the second battle of Moytura.

Manannan Mac Lir (Son of Ler) :[10] husband of *Fand* ("Gentle," as epithet for "Tear") and most popular of Irish gods, equipped with such apparatus as a Cauldron of Truth, a Helmet of Invisibility, and the two famous swords—"Great Fury" and "Little Fury"; anciently portrayed as leading his followers in a chariot over the sea and as king of the Land of the Young; according to one tradition (memorialized in the Manx halfpenny), three-legged, rolling wheel-like on his legs when on land. The Isle of Man (*Inish Manann*) may have been named after him, though the legendary arguments are both pro and con.

Midach: son of Diancecht; also a physician.

Midir: husband of *Etain,* who, changed into a mortal, married Eochaid, King of Ireland, from whom she had later to be won by Midir in a chess game before being returned to the elf mound of Bri-Leith.[11]

Mórrigu (or *Mórrigan*:? "Queen of Apparitions," or *Badb*: "Scald-Crow") : any one of the three horrible war-goddesses —*Anann* (*Ana*), *Bodb* (*Badb*), and *Macha*: would appear during battle in shape of carrion crow or revolting hag in order to feast on the slain. Donahue[12] thinks these war-goddesses "and the valkyries were the results of a common Celto-Germanic development" out of an Indo-European inheritance.

Ogma (or *Ogmios*) : the old and bald "patron of Eloquence and Literature" and fabled inventor of *ogam*; described by the second-century Greek Lucian as wearing the skin of a lion and carrying a club.

---

[10] Cf. D. B. Spaan, "The Place of Mannan Mac Lir in Irish Mythology," *Folklore,* LXXVI (Autumn 1965), 176–95.

[11] *See The Courtship of Etain,* IV, C, 1, and appended fn.

[12] C. Donahue, "The Valkyries and the Irish War-Goddesses," *PMLA,* LVI, 1–12. Cf. W. M. Hennessy, "The Ancient Irish Goddess of War," *Revue Celtique,* I, 32. The Mórrigu appears in W. B. Yeats's *Death of Cuchulain.*

Of course, the Irish recognized numerous other minor divinities and fairy folk, both pleasant and fearsome, including mischievous and elusive specimens like the *leprechán* (< *luchorpán: lu*, "little" + *corpán*, itself a diminutive of *corp*, "body"), or fairy shoemaker, with his secret knowledge of the whereabouts of a hidden crock of gold;[13] and the *puca* (?<O. Norse *púki:* "imp"; cp. Eng. "Puck"), introduced by the Danes but soon acclimated![14]

Whatever their other superstitions, it is apparent[15] that the early Irish believed in numerous fetishes which could be propitiated or coerced, and thus controlled—to the avoidance of threatened evil or even the centering thereof on another. For example, bones or pebbles might be used magically to induce madness or love; the sun, planets, and elements were counted especially powerful as fetishes, as were written letters—conceivably from the association with death (or—perhaps appropriately—learning) implicit in engraving on burial stones. Record, who discusses these matters in detail and whose speculations I am here following, recalls that in Britain even scrapings from Irish books were, mixed with water, regarded as a remedy for snakebite; he even finds some reason for suspecting totemism in the Irish taboos on killing and eating certain animals—for fear of devouring an ancestor!

In general association with festishistic beliefs may be recalled the occasional practice of burying warriors

---

13 See James Stephens' *The Crock of Gold*—and any number of popular Irish stories, *e.g.*, those of Seumas O'Kelly's *Leprechaun of Killmeen*.
14 There is a delightful "pooka" in Ella Young's *Unicorn with Silver Shoes*. See S. Ó. Súilleabháin, *A Handbook of Irish Folklore* (Dublin, 1942). Flann O'Brien's *At Swim-Two-Birds* has "the Pooka Mac Phellimey."
15 Cf. Record, *op. cit.*, Ch. VIII.

armed, erect, and facing the foe,[16] and of carrying dead men into battle: both by way of trying to halt the enemy; the supposedly fearful potency of satires and lampoons, paralleled in some degree—in later times—by that of clerical maledictions;[17] the curious institution of *geasa* (in a sense, taboos),[18] apparently imposed by formula and either injunctional or prohibitive in character; and the amusing practice of fasting[19] (as a threat of suicide—and ghostly vengeance) in attempts at distraint—not to mention the reciprocal practice of "counter-fasting." Indeed, Irish saints are supposed sometimes even to have fasted against God—though whether their actions stimulated any counter-fasting does not appear to be recorded.

Certain writers, it may be remarked in conclusion, seem satisfied to refer to the religion of the early Irish merely as "Druidism,"[20] though of Druidism we know precious little, despite the fact that as early as 200 B.C. Greek merchants had apparently found it operative in Gaul, where indeed Caesar discovered the druids sharing the government with the aristocratic classes as a privileged order (under an elected arch-druid) of philosophers, teachers, soothsayers, and assistants in sacrifices involving the burning of human beings put into wickerwork figures: an order which taught the transmigration of souls

---

[16] The old Irish practiced both cremation with urn-burial and (for the nobility) burial in chambered tumuli.—On burial customs in general, see E. O'Curry, *On the Manners and Customs of the Ancient Irish* (3 vols., ed. with intro. vol. by W. L. Sullivan: London, Dublin, & New York, 1873), and P. W. Joyce, *A Social History of Ancient Ireland* (3d edn., 2 vols.: Dublin & London, 1920), II, 539 ff.

[17] Cf. J. M. Synge, *The Tinker's Wedding.*

[18] Cf. J. R. Reinhard, *The Survival of Geis in Mediæval Romance* (Halle, 1933).

[19] Cf. Yeats's *The King's Threshold,* and see M. Dillon, *The Archaism of Irish Tradition, Procs. of the Brit. Acad.,* Vol. XXXIII.

[20] Cf. T. D. Kendrick, *The Druids* (London, 1927).

(and incidentally permitted the marriage of its professional exponents), and an order whose practices were
continued in secrecy when prohibited by the Romans.
Dalton,[21] referring to Strabo's remark that the Continental Celts had bards, *vates,* and druids, thinks "The
Irish Druids apparently combined the functions of the
Celtic Druids and the Celtic *Vates*"; while Eleanor Hull
maintains,[22] "One thing that is certain is that they worshipped the elements: the earth, the sun, and the wind"—
and swore by them. De Blacam[23] is equally sure the druids
represented a "learned caste" which originated either in
Anglesey or in Ireland and "ruled the spiritual life of the
race, although it was not a priesthood . . ." With the latter
part of this view Joyce,[24] referring to the ninth of
O'Curry's *Lectures on the Manuscript Materials of Ancient Irish History* (Dublin, 1861), seems in accord: "The
ancient Irish druids do not appear to have been *priests* in
any sense of the word. They were . . . magicians, neither
more nor less . . ."

B. General Considerations[25]

Much remains to be learned in the province of immediate concern, but meanwhile we may reasonably entertain
probabilities rooted in manuscript accounts and inherent in
conditions which were the concern of the so-called

---

[21] J. P. Dalton, "Intro." to 4th edn., *The Poets and Poetry of Munster*
(Dublin, 1925), xxxiii–xxxiv.
[22] *Pagan Ireland,* 82.
[23] A. de Blacam, *A First Book of Irish Literature* (Dublin & Cork, 1935),
4.
[24] P. W. Joyce, *Old Celtic Romances* (1920 printing, 3d edn.: Dublin &
London, 1907; orig. 1879), "Note 3," p. 457.
[25] In the present section I have drawn very freely on Dr. Record's *Sociological Study . . . (cit.)* in particular. Cf. Greene, "Early Irish Society,"
in cited book of that title ed. by Dillon.

"Brehon Laws," these latter being—according to tradition
—digests of the laws approved by St. Patrick and his followers, a circumstance making them contemporary in codification with the original Salic Law of the Franks. And
in this connection one may immediately notice that property in general (including slaves, household appurtenances,
and cattle) was in ownership mainly individual—private
even in marriage, as the famous bedroom argument between Queen Medb and her husband emphasizes! Nor did
personal wealth fail to bring social distinction even in
these primitive times. Land-ownership alone, it seems, was
less certainly individual: was probably shared among family or tribal members. Prior, at least, to the latter seventh
century, pastures appear to have been undivided, with each
family allowed to cultivate as much land as it was able.
Poor farmers received—outright or in loan—cattle from
their chieftains in exchange for personal vassalage, which
might imply military service, farm labor, and the sharing
of responsibility for the entertainment of visiting chiefs—
though there were degrees of vassalage, dependent on
size of indebtedness. For the rest, it would seem clearest
to assemble, in summary fashion and under general heads,
the most pertinent knowledge available.

Food: The fact that venison was considered a kingly
food leads to the reflection that the Irish were great hunt-
ers—this despite some evidence of a belief in lycanthropy.
Meats were roasted on peeled hazel spits, boiled in bronze
cauldrons, griddle-broiled, or baked in a pit of hot stones.
Normally, roasting meat was honey-basted; and honey
was also mixed with milk or eaten in the comb—all this
accounting for the importance of apiculture. Favorite
meats included beef, pork, mutton, badger, hare, and
togmall (a rodent like a squirrel) ; preferred fish was sal-

mon—netted, speared, or caught in community weirs;
birds and their eggs (in fact, all eggs) were regarded as
delicacies.

As for vegetables—the Irish preferred cabbage, leeks,
onions, watercress, and nettles; not to mention garlic and
dulse[26] (a delicacy: coarse red seaweed: gathered from
coastal rocks). They had few fruits, but prized apples;
and they valued nut trees, especially the hazel. They also
ate griddle-cakes and "stir-about," a porridge made of
wheat or barley and new milk, or of oatmeal and butter-
milk: to this mixture honey was added for a king's son,
fresh butter for a chieftain, and salt butter for the socially
inferior.

Ale made from barley malt was a favorite drink—and
even carried by the wagonload on cattle raids; mead
(from honey) was another preference. (Wine was apparently not used in earliest times, but was later imported.)

Houses and Building in General: Master-builders had
to understand both carpentry and stonework, though only
dry masonry was known prior to Patrick's coming; lime,
mortar, and Roman arches accompanied Christianity.
Buildings (like vehicles) were mostly of wood, yew (often
carved) being preferred for houses and furniture, as ash
was preferred for spear handles. (Yew, mountain ash,
and hazel were regarded as sacred: with oak, holly, pine,
and apple, they represented "chieftain" trees.)

Pre-Christian houses were mostly cylindrical (though
the banquet halls of Tara and Emania were rectangular):
wickerwork affairs, with osiers or hazel-wattles woven
about driven poles, outer surfaces clay-plastered[27] and

---

[26] As reminiscent, cf. the reference in the O'Kelly-Markievicz play,
Lustre.
[27] One recalls Yeats's *Lake Isle of Innisfree.*

whitewashed, and roofs made of thatched straw or rushes; a door and a roof hole were the only openings. Some houses were, however, made of planks; and glass windows were known. In the rectangular houses, at least, it is believed, lamps hung from a ridge pole over the main apartment. If a building had more than one room, each one had a door to the outside, but there was seldom inside communication. Wooden batons in wall-niches served as knockers; floors were strewn with rushes or straw; and one-apartment houses had sleeping cubicles in the rear. Homesteads, incidentally, were protected by one or more trenches and earth (or stone) ramparts. These trenches might be moats—possibly supplemented by monoliths and palisades of stakes linked by interwoven withes and crested with thorn.[28]

Domestic Implements, etc.: These included reaping hooks of bronze or (later) iron and various household utensils of wood, metal, or clay. Vats, buckets, and the like were usually made of beech or yew; drinking horns, of bullock horns ornamented with precious metals.

Craftsmanship: Metallurgy was highly developed, gold being abundant: indeed, it has been claimed metalworking was introduced into Ireland *c.* 2000 B.C.! Copper, silver, iron, zinc, lead, and coal were mined; bronze was made of copper and tin—reddish or whitish according to relative proportions, the whitish (perhaps the alloy known as *findruine*) being used for the finer work. There were blacksmiths, working in iron to mold swords, spearheads,

---

28 Kerry and other areas of western Ireland preserve some low stone huts, often with surrounding walls (*raths*) ; these *cloghans* are unmortared and "bee-hive" in shape. A group of *cloghans* (the main dwelling called the *tech mór*) encircled by a *rath,* or *lis,* would constitute a *cathair,* or fort.— A living-site located in a lake or bog was known as a *crannog.* (Cf. W. G. Wood-Martin, *The Lake-Dwellings of Ireland:* London & Dublin, 1886.)

and domestic ware—an important class, often regarded as magicians, seers, and prophets, their forges centers of gossip; similarly, there were braziers and gold- and silversmiths.

Clothing was made of wool and linen—and often dyed black, saffron, blue, crimson, or purple by the women, a man's presence during the dyeing being considered unlucky. Embroidering (with colored threads and leather design patterns) and sewing (with woolen thread and steel- or bronze-eyed needles) were leading occupations among upper-class women.

Leather (tanned with oak or apple bark and thong-stitched) was used for shoes, bags, jackets, bottles, book covers, and wallets—not to mention the satchels, frequently ornamented, in which manuscripts (some of them exquisitely illuminated) were kept. Incidentally, a master craftsman enjoyed high social rank; and a finished object had to be blessed by the artificer and the first other person to see it.

Dress, Ornamentation, etc.: Men might wear long tight trousers fastened underfoot or a sort of kilt, with cloaks, jackets, and capes (often with hoods). Women wore a sleeved kirtle under a cloak or long tunic—and underwear. It was common to see girdles dangling a purse or fitted with pockets, as well as gemmed and valuable metal ornaments, often of fine workmanship: finger- and arm-rings, neck-torques, crescents, brooches, golden balls for hair-ends, etc. Shoes and sandals were of leather, silver, or bronze. Men generally went bareheaded, and rank was denoted by the number of colors in one's dress: according to legend, kings and queens were allowed seven, poets and doctors, six; etc. Among the blond, aristocratic Celts, both men and women plaited and braided their hair around the head, the men also wearing long beards. Bathing (in large tubs of water heated with hot stones)—with soap and anointing oils—was common, warriors being bathed by women. Women dyed their nails crimson, caring for them and their hands meticulously; they also darkened their eyebrows with berry juice.

Transportation and Trade: Roads existed in Ireland from about the second century of the Christian era onward, permitting chariots (two-wheeled and two-horsed) to be used in transportation as well as in hunting and fighting.[29] For water-travel, hollowed-log canoes and curraghs (made of varying thicknesses of hide stretched over wicker frames) were utilized. There were even seagoing curraghs, strongly built of tanned leather and provided with sturdy ribs, decks, seats, masts, and oars. They facilitated Irish emigration to Wales and Scotland during the fourth and fifth centuries.

The Irish apparently had some foreign trade[30] in remotely early times and a great deal during the fifth century. They employed barter, no Irish coinage apparently antedating the tenth century; and they imported many slaves from England.

Domestic Animals: The Irish regarded the herding of cattle, swine, goats, and sheep as more important than tillage; cows, bulls, and oxen were their most valuable possessions, cattle being "a measure of wealth and a medium of exchange,"[31] with red-eared white cows espe-

---

[29] Cf. J. O'B. Crowe, "The Irish Chariot," *Jour. of the Royal Hist. and Archeo. Ass'n of Ireland,* Fourth Ser., I (Dublin, 1878), 413–31.

[30] Cf. H. Zimmer, "Über direkte Handelsverbindungen Westgalliens mit Irland im Altertum und frühen Mittelalter," *Sitz. d. k. preuss. Akad. d. Wissensch.,* 1909 and 1910.

[31] Record, *op. cit.,* 108.—A slave woman, *e.g.,* was "worth three cows or five head of horned cattle" (Hull, *Pagan Ireland,* 35). Incidentally, captives automatically became slaves.

cially valuable and pigs second in importance to cattle. In fact, pigs—with sheep—were regarded as hearthside companions.[32]

Cats were used for mousing, and there were many dogs: cattle-, watch-, hunting-, and lap-dogs. Some hounds are said to have been as large as small horses; when not chasing game, these followed the hunter's chariot. Mad dogs were killed; and after their bodies had been burnt, the ash was thrown into a stream.

Horses, which ran wild in mountain pastures, were used with chariots and carts, in packing and racing. Record[33] recalls that "as one Irish writer puts it, there were no asses in Ireland before the English occupation."

Marital and Family Practices:[34] The Irish apparently came early to the practice of monogyny, though there is evidence of other types of marriage: *e.g.,* like the first-century Continental Celts, the Irish may have practiced sharing a wife among brothers, and there are other signs of group rights to women (as among the Fenians). What is more, there was probably concubinage, according to degree of wealth. The *jus primae noctis* was common; and hosts[35] had to furnish wives or daughters to the bed of the king (or his son, or his poet) when he was on circuit.

In general, a patriarchal organization, as common among Aryans, obtained, though women enjoyed high legal and social standing, with their own property rights and "courts of appeal." They had separate houses—

---

[32] And cf. Liam O'Flaherty's *Skerrett.*
[33] *Op. cit.,* 110.
[34] Cf. de Jubainville's articles in *Revue Archéologique* (n.s.), XLII, 331–34, and *Revue Celtique,* XXV, 1–16 and 181–207; VII, 91–96. But note also Frank O'Connor's preface to *Kings, Lords, & Commons* (New York: Knopf, 1959), viii.
[35] Cf. the opening of James Stephens' *Deirdre.*

grianáns ("sunny chambers")—and often fought as warriors beside their husbands, though the Abbot Adamnan
is credited with ending this practice at the beginning of the
eighth century. Incidentally, the six "womanly gifts" were
listed as beauty, singing, sweet speech, needlework, wis-
dom, and chastity. The last of these was considered especially desirable in the daughters of rich or important
men.

Daughters of a given family were generally married off
according to age (cf. the situation in Cuchulainn's wooing
of Emer), and a bride-price was customary: not the
Roman dowry, but a payment *for* the bride to her father
or—if the father were dead and she had a brother, to him.
There was also a marriage gift to the bride (whereby
Ness got Fergus originally to give Concobar the kingship
for a year).

In general, courtship depended on arrangement rather
than romance, though abductions and elopements were
common; betrothal brought a feast—and cohabitation,
marriage following presently, though perhaps not until
childbirth had occurred. The wedding itself might consist
merely of bedding before witnesses after the betrothal—
or might involve feasting; among the Fenians a woman
was passed from warrior to warrior before reaching her
husband. Frequently a druid would name an auspicious
day for marriage (Monday, Tuesday, and Wednesday
were considered lucky for women; Thursday, Friday, and
Sunday, for men; Saturdays, for both).

The early Irish apparently practiced one-year trial mar-
riages, and separation was easy for both sides by repudia-
tion; but there was high regard for children, especially
sons, with fines for abortion and with infanticide rare and
abhorrent. Curious beliefs obtained: *e.g.,* that magical

pregnancy might result from swallowing something, or "that coition with three men brought about the birth of triplets"[36]; and there may be some hints of the *couvade*, unless Frank O'Connor is correct in blaming this suspicion on erroneous etymology.

Childbirth usually took place in isolation—perhaps in a forest or garden, the mother being in some instances attended by a maid; and it was counted lucky to strike a child's head against stone while giving birth—or directly afterward. A newborn child was formally presented to the father, or to some other male relative; and children were often put out to nurse or placed with foster parents. We don't know what explains the fosterage, of which a special sort was "literary fosterage" under a *fili* or *brehon*, who in such case had a claim on his pupil's aid during any time of need throughout life.

As early as possible, a boy was taught games, sheepherding, and the rudiments of warfare. At seven a child might be legally classified as "a fool or a sensible person"; boys could be knighted and take up arms at this age, and might be sent away for instruction in warfare. Girls were considered eligible for marriage at sixteen or seventeen; boys, about the same age or a little later. Sons belonged wholly to fathers until granted emancipation;[37] indeed, it would seem that fathers had *absolute power* over all children, that deformed or frail children were sometimes killed, and that girls in particular were occasionally exposed to die: nevertheless, both sons and daughters were expected to care for aged parents. There was much ille-

---

[36] Record, *op. cit.*, 229.—Cf. A. Lang, *Myth, Ritual, and Religion,* II, 23 ff. (London, 1887; edn. 1913); F. Lot, "Les Guérriers d'Ulster en Mal d'Enfants," *Annales de Bretagnes,* XI, 151-52.

[37] Cf. the modern reminiscence of this tradition in Synge's *Playboy of the Western World.*

gitimacy, even though bastards lived under a stigma; but there has been discovered no evidence whatsoever of paid prostitution.

Sports, Amusements, and Public Assemblies[38]: Aside from hunting and fishing (not to mention fighting!), the most common Irish sports included swimming, wrestling, and hurley (cf. field hockey). A favorite game was *fidchell*—perhaps equivalent to chess. Among public assemblies, the *feis,* or fair, deserves particularization. Remotely originating in the funeral games once celebrated in old burial grounds (as commemorative events, advisable to ensure food, general prosperity, and independence for given kingdoms), it came to be held yearly or triennially and provided a convenient opportunity for pronouncing laws, considering genealogies, exchanging merchandise, holding sports contests (such as horse-racing, its institution attributed to Lugh) and artistic events, etc. The leading one—a seven-day affair—was that of Tara, held at Samhain; other well-known fairs, usually convened 1 August (*Lughnasadh:* "Lugh's commemoration," honoring his foster-mother, Tailltiu), are associated with Uisnech, Taillte, Emain Macha, Cruachan, and Carmen (a triennial assembling celebrated in the *Metrical Dindshenchas:* see E. Gwynn, ed.-trans., Vols. 8-12, Todd Lecture Series, Royal Irish Academy).

Justice and Retribution: Modern agencies of law-enforcement being nonexistent, physical injury, insult, and murder were compensable according to set schedules plus an "honor-price" relative to the injured person's

---

[38] Cf. G. Keating, Comyn-Dinneen trans. of *Forus Feasa ar Éirinn,* I, 221; II, 245 ff. This *History* runs to 4 vols.: London, 1902-14; it was first issued in trans. by D. O'Connor: 1723.—See also J. Dunn, *The Ancient Irish Epic . . . Táin Bó Cuálnge* (London, 1914), 47 ff.; K. Meyer, "Boyish Exploits of Finn," *Ériu,* I, 180 ff.

rank. Venal murder called for revenge by relatives or the payment of *eric* (a fine)—if not directly by the murderer, then by any friends who concealed him or let him escape (in which case he forfeited his property as part of the *eric*). Other practices included the fasting and counter-fasting referred to in the first division of the present section.

It may be added that open dueling and single combat by representative champions of opposing armies (one recalls Cuchulainn and Ferdiad) were approved practices, as were trial by ordeal, collection of the heads of slain warriors, and, in Christian days, penance by drifting help-lessly in a coracle. Anciently, criminals sometimes side-stepped usual patterns of behavior by claiming right of sanctuary of chiefs or *filid* (as, later, of churchmen, who are said often to have abused the privilege of extending it).

IV. THE WILD HERITAGE: LITERATURE PROPER[1]

A. Lanthorn: General Introduction

1. Manuscripts

Aside from the impressive mass of material (in Latin as well as in Irish) dealing with religious, genealogical, annalistic, historical, scientific (including medical), and legalistic subject matter (not to mention translations from Greek, Latin, and other tongues), Irish literature proper consists mostly of lyric verse and prose tales (very frequently studded with passages of verse)—the two categories to be given some attention here. Curiously enough, formal drama *in Irish* older than the minor contributions of Dr. Hyde (born *c.* 1860) appears to be nonexistent; aesthetically, it seems that—subsequent at least to the days of purely oral transmission of literature—the Irish genius favored the *uirscéal* (romance).

The reader may be here reminded that next to nothing of literary value has been preserved in Old Irish, although there are, *e.g.*, some glosses and certain parts of the *Book of the Dun Cow* and the *Book of Armagh* to testify lin-

[1] The student will find useful T. P. Cross's *Motif-Index of Early Irish Literature* (Bloomington: Indiana Univ. Press, 1952), as well as the Thomas Davis lectures edited by Myles Dillon as *Irish Sagas* (Cork: Mercier Press, 1968). For bibliographical guidance, see R. I. Best's *A Bibliography of Irish Philology and of Printed Irish Literature* (Dublin, 1913) and *Bibliography of Irish Philology and Manuscript Literature: Publications 1913–1941* (Dublin, 1942) ; also, A. R. Eager's *A Guide to Irish Bibliographical Material* (London: Library Ass'n, 1964).

guistically to literary activity during at least the latter part of the period in reference, not to mention such relics as the verse of Blathmac, preserved in a seventeenth-century manuscript (see J. Carney, *Early Irish Poetry:* Cork, 1965; 45 ff.). But we are mainly concerned with works of some artistic and aesthetic value, and of these it may be said that, except for the Fenian, or Ossianic, material (most of which is in Modern Irish), the majority of the important manuscripts are extant in Middle Irish. Nevertheless, it is generally felt—despite some scholarly dissent—that the major tales (including the Fenian) are in point of *substance* undatably (except approximately) earlier than the crystallizations *reflected* by preserved specimens. Those crystallizations were possibly—indeed, probably—made during the seventh, eighth, and ninth centuries; they themselves, the original manuscripts, doubtless with numerous transcripts and redactions, have apparently all been lost—or, in conceivable instances, at least hopelessly dispersed: primarily as a result of Danish invasions and the Anglo-Norman occupation, periods of lamentable destruction. Centuries of succeeding trouble have also collected their cultural toll. Many manuscripts were carried abroad, mostly to the continent of Europe: during early ages, by Irish missionaries and scholars; during later penal times, by priests emigrating to safety. Destruction and dispersion have thus left Ireland scarcely a dozen manuscripts predating the opening of the eleventh century, although over fifty (mainly glosses) have been credited to the Continent. Even so, there appears to be extant no manuscript in Irish written prior to the eighth century.

In recording the old pagan tales, a process largely carried out in the monasteries, the scribes and copyists appear-frequently to have modernized the prose phraseology and inserted a few Christian elements (as was more markedly the case with Anglo-Saxon manuscripts in Britain); but though Joyce remarks[2] that they sometimes went so far as to alter "the descriptions of antique customs and equipments so as to bring them into conformity with their own times," it is significant to notice that interspersed verse was mostly left unchanged, probably because of its structural delicacy and extreme obscurity[2a] (general considerations useful in attempts at approximate dating of material). On this whole matter of mixed form, Hyde postulates[3] the following:

> We may take it . . . that in the earliest days the romances were composed in verse and learned by heart by the students—possibly before any alphabet was known at all; afterwards when lacunæ occurred through defective memory on the part of the reciter he filled up the gaps with prose. Those who committed to paper our earliest tales wrote down as much of the old poetry as they could recollect or had access to, and wrote the connecting narrative in prose. Hence it soon came to pass that if a story pretended to any antiquity it had to be interspersed with verses, and at last . . . the Irish taste became so confirmed to this style of writing that authors adopted it . . . even in the seventeenth and eighteenth centuries.

Professor Dillon, however, recalls[4] Oldenberg's opinion that the mixed "is the earliest form of literature known to the Indo-Europeans."

It may next be observed that the bulk of manuscript material remaining to Ireland is now in two Dublin institutions—Trinity College (whose charter of incorporation

---

[2] *Social History* . . . , cit., I, 535.
[2a] Cf. the problem with Sean O'Falvey's MS. in Daniel Corkery's "Clan Falvey" (*The Yellow Bittern and Other Plays,* Dublin and London, 1920).
[3] *Literary History* . . . , cit., 260–61.
[4] M. Dillon, *Early Irish Literature* (Univ. of Chicago Press, 1948), 2.

was granted in 1592) and the Royal Irish Academy (its library founded two years before the Academy was incorporated in 1785). There are miscellaneous other collections, to be sure, both in and out of Ireland; among them may be named those in the Franciscan Library at Merchants' Quay (Dublin), the Armagh Public Library, the National Library of Scotland and the Edinburgh Advocates', the Oxford Bodleian and the British Museum— not to mention certain Continental libraries. Professor Dillon estimates[5] the number of extant Irish manuscripts at perhaps two thousand; the major compilations—*i.e.*, those most interesting from a literary point of view—may be listed as follows:

> *The Book of the Dun Cow* (*Leabhar na h-Uidhre*: oldest preserved compilation: *c.* A.D. 1100; 134 folio pp.—Royal Irish Academy MS. 23.E.25.): transcription from older (?8th century) material made by Maelmuire Mac Ceilechair and a contemporary, with infusions made perhaps two centuries later; some leaves missing, leaving several of its 65 items incomplete; title from tradition that its non-extant original "was written on vellum made from the skin of St. Ciaran's pet cow at Clonmacnoise"[6]; contents include imperfect versions of the *Voyage of Maelduin* and the *Táin Bó Cuálnge,* as well as copies of the *Courtship of Emer,* the *Feast of Bricriu,* the *Abduction of Prince Connla,* etc.— Most of the tales belong to the Ulster Cycle. (Ed. by R. I. Best and O. Bergin as *Lebor na Huidre*: Dublin & London, 1929.)

> *The Book of Leinster,* or *Book of Noughaval* (*Leabhar Laighneach*: pre-1160; 410 folio pp.—Trinity College MS. H.2.18.): nearly 1000 miscellaneous pieces in prose and verse, including a copy of the *Táin Bó Cuálnge,* compiled by Finn Mac Gorman, Bishop of Kildare (†1160).—Ed. R. Atkinson (Oxford, 1880).

[5] *Ibid.,* xviii.
[6] Joyce, *Social History . . . , cit.,* I, 493.—A facsimile of a copy of the MS. made by Joseph O'Longan was published in 1871 by the Royal Irish Academy.

MS. Rawlinson B.502 (Bodleian Library, Oxford; 12th century).

The Book of Ballymote (*Leabhar Baile an Mhota*: end of 14th century; 501 folio pp.—Royal Irish Academy MS. 23.P.12.): compilation out of Sligo in several hands; includes in its prose and verse miscellaneous early historical and romantic tales, a translation of Nennius, and "a history of the most remarkable women of Ireland down to the English invasion"![7]

The Yellow Book of Lecan (*Leabhar Buidhe Lecain*: 14-15th century [sometimes dated *c.* 1390]: *c.* 500 quarto pp.— Trinity College MS. H.2.16.): miscellany of prose and verse containing imperfect copies of the *Voyage of Maelduin* and the *Táin Bó Cuálnge*.

The (Great) Book of Lecan (*Leabhar Mór Lecain*: 1416–18; *c.* 600 pp.—Royal Irish Academy MS. 23.P.2.): suggestive in content of the *Book of Ballymote*.

The Book of Lismore (?1450–1500; discovered 1814 at Castle Lismore, Co. Waterford.—Library of the Duke of Devonshire, Chatsworth, Derbyshire.): contains mostly saints' lives in homily form, but also Ossianic and other material; in several hands.

The Book of Fermoy (MS. somewhat in question as to date— probably 15th century—and real title.—Royal Irish Academy MS. 23.E.29.): miscellany variously compiled; contains mythological and legendary matter of interest.

With the foregoing may be mentioned two other Royal Irish Academy folios of unusual importance: *The Book of Hy Many* (14-15th century) and the *Leabhar Brecc* (14th century).

2. The *Filid* and Associated Classes

Traditionally, of course, the prose tales and verse which are our major concern have been regarded as the productions of *fili* and *bard,* the former "a man fully qualified and certificated in all the branches of a Gaelic

---

[7] Joyce, *ibid.,* 496.

liberal education,"[8] who "might practise in any one of the three professions, Law, History, Poetry . . ."[9] In respect of the last instance it may be recalled that the ancient Irish distinguished between poetry (*ecsi*) and bard-craft (*bairdne*), the *filid* being the aristocratic practitioners of the former as the bards (*baird*) were the humbler exponents of the latter, though the *filid* supposedly often left the delivery of their own verse to bards or others.

In any event, it is clear that the *filid* constituted a highly privileged and well-organized body, given to making official tours during which their learning won many rich rewards from the kings and chieftains visited. Supported by the populace, and much feared for their often-vented satiric power and its supposed magical effects,[10] they are said to have abused their privileges shamefully and eventually to have been judged for banishment at the Convention of Druim-Cetta (A.D. 575), only to be so well defended by St. Colum Cille (himself a member of the order) as to be given instead regulation, with a reduction in rights and possible exactions.

The *filid*, who grouped themselves around masters, demanded of recruits a strict scholastic training[11]; indeed,

[8] Dalton, "Intro.," *Poets and Poetry of Munster,* edn. *cit.,* xxxi.

[9] *Ibid.,* xxxiii. Dillon (*The Cycles of the Kings:* Oxford, 1946: p. 116), a discrimination of the annalists obviously in mind, speaks of *"brethemuin* and *senchaidi,* filid whose special studies were law and history respectively."—Incidentally, the *Annals of the Kingdom of Ireland* were edited and translated by J. O'Donovan (Dublin, 1856).

[10] See F. N. Robinson, "Satirists and Enchanters in Early Irish Literature," in *Studies in the History of Religions* . . . (New York, 1912), 95–130; J. Travis, "A Druidic Prophecy, the First Irish Satire, and a Poem to Raise Blisters," *PMLA,* LVII, 909–15; and M. C. Randolph, "Celtic Smiths and Satirists: Partners in Sorcery," *E. L. H.,* VIII, 184–97. (Material of consonant interest may be found in the last-named author's "Female Satirists of Ancient Ireland," *So. Folklore Qu.,* VI, 75–87.)

[11] The schools of *filid* were apparently succeeded by "Bardic Schools," which in Ireland seem to have persisted well into the seventeenth century, though their Scotch counterparts lasted into the eighteenth. The

they were ranked by grade according to their years of such training, with the satisfaction of certain set requirements. Thus, an *ollamh* (or "doctor" in *filedecht*), representing the highest grade, must have had twelve years of training and mastered 350 tales (250 "prime," 100 "secondary"), aside from other qualifications. (It is Hyde's reasonable suggestion[12] that these folk did not have to memorize tales word for word, but had instead to master sequences of events, to be filled out individually during the actual telling of stories.) It is interesting to observe that an *ollamh* ordained by king or chieftain ranked second only to such a one at table and enjoyed amazing privileges for himself and his retinue.—Below the *ollamh* ranged the lesser orders of *filid,* from *anruth* to *drisiuc,* the latter of whom was required to be master of only twenty tales. Nor is it uninteresting to find that there were also grades of musicians, the *ollamh* among these being required to be able to perform perfectly the *Suantraighe*—a slumber-bringing strain, the *Goltraighe*— a strain inducing tears, and the *Geantraighe*—a strain evoking laughter. One should add that the bards proper had their own classifications: there was that of *saer-baird,* with seven grades, ranging from *rig-* (or "king") *bard* to *bo-* (or "cow") *bard;* and that of *daer-baird,* a lower order also of seven grades. The *filid,* who may have lost something of their former status during the Scandinavian invasions, were after the Anglo-Norman invasion succeeded by the professional bards, frequently retainers of

tradition may be said to have been carried on in a sense by the modern hedge-teachers (cf. Padraic Colum's "Poor Scholar of the Forties" in *Wild Earth*) and itinerant masters and bards.—One may cf. G. Murphy, "Bards and Filidh," *Éigse,* II, 200; D. Corkery, "The Bardic Schools," in *The Hidden Ireland* (Dublin, 1925); P. J. Dowling, *The Hedge Schools of Ireland* (Cork: Mercier Press, 1968).
[12] *Literary History . . . , cit.,* Ch. XXII.

given families for varying periods of time. It was these later bards, codifiers of Irish metrics, who in Quiggin's view[13] were probably responsible for the development of "the Ossianic cycle" and the composition of "many, if not all, of the heroic ballads dealing with Finn and his warriors."

3. Story "Lists"

Of the tales[14] which were once the delight of the *filid* and their fellows various classifying "lists" (recalling originals dating back to perhaps the seventh century) have been made, as for example in the *Book of Leinster;* Joyce records[15] the categories in this fashion:

> Classes of Prime Stories:—1. Battles: 2. *Imrama,* Navigations, or Voyages [Most celebrated and influential]: 3. Tragedies: 4. Adventures: 5. Cattle-raids (or Preyings): 6. Hostings or Military Expeditions: 7. Courtships: 8. Elopements: 9. Caves or Hidings (*i.e.* adventures of persons hiding for some reason in caves or other remote places): 10. Destructions (of palaces, &c.): 11. Sieges or Encampments: 12. Feasts: 13. Slaughters.
>
> Classes of Minor Stories: 14. Pursuits: 15. Visions [Second in type-popularity]: 16. Exiles, or Banishments: 17. Lake Eruptions.

---

13 E. Quiggin, "Prolegomena to the Study of the Later Irish Bards 1200–1500," *Procs. of the British Acad.,* 1911–12 (Oxford), 89 ff. Quotations from p. 93.

14 A most valuable collection of miscellaneous translations is *Ancient Irish Tales,* ed. T. P. Cross and C. H. Slover (New York, 1936). Cf. also the translations of P. W. Joyce in *Old Celtic Romances* (orig. London, 1879; latest rpt., Dublin, 1966) and those of S. H. O'Grady in *Silva Gadelica* (London, 1892); *v.,* further, such volumes as *Anecdota from Irish Manuscripts* (ed. and trans. J. O'Donovan: Dublin, 1856), *Heroic Romances of Ireland* (tr. A. H. Leahy: London, 1905–06), *Hero Tales of Ireland* (ed. J. Curtin: London, 1894), *Legendary Fictions of the Irish Celts* (coll. by P. Kennedy: London, 1891), etc.—Cf. R. Thurneysen, *Sagen aus dem alten Irland* (Berlin, 1901).—Miscellaneous re-creations may be found in the author's *Carved in Findruine* (Philadelphia, 1969).

15 *Social History . . . ,* cit., I, 533.

Still in Joyce's phraseology,[16] "only the four highest grades of poets [*i.e., ollamh, anruth, clí,* and *cana*] . . . were permitted to tell both the prime and the minor stories: the lower grades were confined to the chief stories." Of course, many tales, as indicated before, are now lost, though between five and six hundred appear to be extant; so long ago as 1899 Alfred Nutt estimated[17] that "There exists a mass of Irish romantic literature which if printed would fill some two to three thousand octavo pages, known to be older than the eleventh century [*i.e.,* as to *substance*] . . ." Many of the tales have long since been noticed to correspond with ancient Greek and Oriental stories; some of the most popular ones—the "visions" and "voyages"[18]—supposedly belong to the seventh and eighth centuries, among the "visions" being the crazily satiric one attributed to Mac Conglinne and extant in a Middle Irish version, among the *imrama* being the famous *Voyages* of Bran and Maelduin.[19] These representative tales are summarized below.

The Vision of Mac Conglinne: Anier Mac Conglinne says he made this work to exorcise a "demon of gluttony" from the throat of King Cathal of Munster, a contender for the High Kingship against Fergal of Ailech, whose

---

16 *Ibid.*
17 "Celtic and Medieval Romance." *Popular Studies in Mythology, Romance and Folklore,* No. 1 (London, 1899), p. 27.
18 See Meyer-Nutt edn., *Voyage of Bran, cit.,* and St. John D. Seymour's *Irish Visions of the Otherworld* (London, 1920).
19 Cf. that of St. Brendan (voyage perhaps made *c.* sixth century; see O'Curry, *Lectures on the Manuscript Materials of Ancient Irish History* [Dublin, 1861], 289) ; a more tiresomely recorded "voyage" is that of the sons of O'Corra (R.I.A. MS.: *Book of Fermoy:* see O'Curry, *ibid.;* text translated by W. Stokes, *Revue Celtique,* XIV (Jan. 1893) ; earlier tr. by Joyce, *Old Celtic Romances).—*K. Meyer translated the *Vision of Mac Conglinne (Aislinge Meic Conglinne—*main recension in *Leabhar Brecc:* London, 1892).

sister Ligach loved Cathal. (Having ascertained that Ligach was sending Cathal fruit, sweets, etc., Fergal had some of these gifts bewitched so that the demon of gluttony formed in Cathal's throat.)

Mac Conglinne then tells how he, a scholar at Armagh, decided to change scholarship for poetry and seek Cathal, in whose company he expected to get food: how he went to Cork, found a bug-infested guesthouse, refused the Abbot Manchin's proffered "whey-water," and satirized Cork food, thus gaining from the abbot a beating with whips, a soaking in the Lee, a night of naked discomfort, and an order for crucifixion.

We next learn how, by one dodge or another, Mac Conglinne stayed his promised execution till next day and how, as he stood tied naked to a stone by night, an angel came with a vision which he shaped in verse; how in the morning he satirically carried Manchin's pedigree back *through foods* to Abel and Adam, related his vision of foods, and was sent to Cathal by Manchin, who said he had had a revelation that the vision was to cure the king. The rest of the long, overexuberant, and somewhat silly tale (which satirizes the Church as well as gluttony) explains how Mac Conglinne impudently forced the king to fast, exorcised the demon (who was tempted out of Cathal's mouth by food and the satirist's talk of delicacies, had the house burnt down around him, but in the end escaped), and won a great reward—including Abbot Manchin's valued cloak.

The Voyage of Bran:[20] Febal's son, Bran, whose name means "Crow," is put to sleep by faery music and awakens

---

[20] For MSS., trans., etc., see Meyer-Nutt edn., *cit.;* oldest fragment in *Book of the Dun Cow.*

to find a white-blossomed silver branch near him; he takes
the branch into the royal *dun,* full of kingly guests, and a
strange woman appears to sing "fifty quatrains" to him.
Her song, offered as a lure to Bran, tells of a marvelous
island paradise called Emne, supported by four pillars
in the sea; it also contains a curious prophecy of Christ's
advent. At its conclusion, the silver branch leaps from
Bran's to the hand of the woman, who disappears with it.

Next morning Bran takes to sea with twenty-seven
men. He meets Manannan Mac Lir, who—in thirty quatrains—says he is en route to Ireland to father Mongán
(but also works some theological reference into his song!)
and prophesies Bran's arrival at Emne, "Land of
Women," before sunset.

Bran comes first to the "Island of Joy," to which he
sends a crew member—who straightway becomes one of
its people. At Emne, Bran is welcomed by the chief
woman, who draws his coracle ashore by tossing a ball of
thread which adheres to the palm of his hand (one recalls
a similar device in the *Voyage of Maelduin*). For centuries (though it seems only a year) Bran and his company
enjoy the immortal pleasures of the isle; when homesickness recalls them to Ireland, the chief woman, prophesying regret on their part, warns them not to touch land,
but tells them to pick up their comrade on the Isle of Joy.
Off Srub Brain,[21] Bran identifies himself—to be unrecognized, but told his "Voyage" is part of the people's ancient
story lore. One man jumps ashore—and turns to ashes on
touching the soil. Bran then tells his story, says farewell,
and departs on unknown voyagings.

---

21 "Raven's Beak," w. Ireland: see *The Tragic Death of Curoi Mac Dairi*
(cf. R. Thurneysen, *Die Irische Helden- und Königsage* [Halle, 1921]).—
Cf. R. D. Joyce's *Blanid* (1879).

The Voyage of Maelduin:[22] Maelduin's father is slain
by coastal raiders, and the widow takes her later-born son
for safety to her friend the queen, who rears him as one
of her own children. When Maelduin, as a young man,
learns his true parentage, he returns to his father's territory, from which he subsequently (after ascertaining the
whereabouts of the raiders' fleet) sets out to avenge his
father's death. A druid advises him on the building of his
curragh and sets sixty men as the number of its crew. But
(to save these persistent three foster brothers from
drowning) he adds the queen's sons: so ill luck follows,
beginning with a storm that prevents him from avenging
himself on his father's murderer at the first island he
reaches.

Allowing the curragh to drift, Maelduin and his crew,
sometimes suffering hunger and thirst, come on a long
series of wonders, mostly in the shape of marvelous is-
lands (some fixed, like that of the animals lucent with internal fire, some of the disappearing variety).—On the
Island of the Cat a foster brother is slain by the animal
for trying to steal a torque after general hospitality has
been enjoyed; a second foster brother is lost on the Island
of Weeping; and the third disappears on the Island of
Laughing. No particular logic seems to govern the number
and character of the adventures sustained; eventually a
penitent hermit on a sea rock foretells the wanderers'
return home, but warns Maelduin to forgive the man who
slew his father. In due time the voyagers reach the island
of Maelduin's old enemies, whence the storm had blown
them at the beginning of their adventures. Maelduin is

---

22 MSS.: *Yellow Book of Lecan,* Brit. Museum *MS. Harleian 5280, Book
of the Dun Cow* (imperfect), *et al.* O'Curry dates the voyage *c.* A.D. 700.
Trans. W. Stokes, *Revue Celtique,* IX, X; Joyce, *Old Celtic Romances.*

welcomed; peace obtains; and the wanderers relate their story before returning to Ireland. (Tennyson based a flabby ballad on Joyce's translation of this "voyage.")

It may be added that in Ireland, as elsewhere, some of the saints' lives were injected with the elements of lively romance; but present purposes do not demand consideration of these relics.[23]

B. Mercury: Lyric Material and Verse-Form[24]

Lyrical verse in Irish, though traditionally regarded as beginning with the gnomic Amergin, a son of Milesius, and despite the claims made for it by certain extravagant —if not fanatic—admirers, presents none too impressive a history except from a mathematical point of view; the great burst of incomparable Irish lyricism came in English during late- and post-Victorian "Renaissance" times. Everything considered, early Irish verse[25]—which, oddly enough, contains relatively few out-and-out love poems— seems most significant in certain nature lyrics, eulogies

---

23 Concerned readers may consult C. Plummer's ed. and trans. *Vitae Sanctorum Hiberniae* (2 v.: Oxford, 1910) or the same author's *Lives of the Irish Saints* (Oxford, 1922).

24 Cf. especially Dillon, *Early Irish Literature, cit.,* Ch. VIII; S. Gwynn, *Irish Literature and Drama* (London, 1936), Ch. II; Hyde, *Literary History . . . , cit.,* Ch. XXXIX; K. Jackson, *Studies in Early Celtic Nature Poetry* (Cambridge Univ. Press, 1935); S. O'Faoláin (ed)., *The Silver Branch* (New York, 1938); Quiggin, *op. cit.;* G. Sigerson (ed.), *Bards of the Gael and Gall* (3d edn., Dublin & London, 1925); J. Vendryes, *La Poésie de cour en Irlande et en Galles* (Paris, 1932); E. Knott, *An Introduction to Irish Syllabic Poetry . . . 1200–1600* (Cork & Dublin, 1928); O. Bergin, "On the Origin of Modern Irish Rhythmical Verse," *Mélanges linguistiques . . .* (Copenhagen, 1937); G. Murphy, *Early Irish Lyrics* (Oxford, 1956); R. Flower, *The Irish Tradition* (Oxford, 1947); F. O'Connor (ed.-tr.), *Kings, Lords & Commons* (New York, 1959); J. Carney, ed., *Early Irish Poetry* (Cork, 1965).

25 Flower, *op. cit.,* 68, calls Fland mac Lonain (?†893), a Connachtman, "the first professional poet of Ireland of whom we have any definite tradition."

(the earliest reportedly out of Leinster and Munster),
elegiac verses, and historical items; and while many may
be content to endorse Sigerson's claim[26] that "bardic
poetry was characterized by classic reserve in thought,
form, and expression," there will always remain not a few
to whom "reserve" is not a sufficient recommendation—
readers inclined to agree with O'Faoláin's admission, di-
rect or tacit, that these verses were generally lacking in
"any sense of total form" and were (whether because of
the Bardic Schools, racial traditionalism, or what not)
representative of the "technically admirable," but little
else. Considerable encomiastic verse (sociologically indica-
tive but aesthetically inconsequential) appeared (as did
religious[27]—not a little of this latter bearing a medieval
Latin signet, impressed either directly or indirectly
through translation) from the seventh century to the
early seventeenth—the latter a century which can boast
little that is more significant than such disputatious matter
as that assembled in *The Contention of the Poets* and such
miscellaneous verse as that of David O'Bruidair, though
it produced (as did the eighteenth) numerous narrative
pieces concerned with the Fenian tradition popularized
by the Bardic Schools, such as the Ossianic ballads often
characterized—as Hyde observed—by semidramatic
opening dialogues between Oisin and St. Patrick (familiar
to modern readers through Yeats's *Wanderings of Oisin*).
The eighteenth century brought also much patriotic versi-
fying, beneath contempt as poetry, with more individual
work represented by nothing more exciting perhaps than
Brian MacGiolla Meidhre's *The Midnight Court* (*c.*

---

[26] Intro., *op. cit.*, 23.
[27] *E.g.*, that of the thirteenth-century Donnchadh Mór Ó Dálaigh, the
leading medieval Irish religious poet.

1780); thereafter came the sporadic effusions of the "hedge schoolmasters" concerned with imitating the ancient satire of the *filid* or augmenting the never-sparse supply of patriotic and religious songs. Incidentally, it has been maintained that many "poems" in late Irish are probably to be properly ascribed to very early poets, the language of the verses having changed with the periods of transmission; meanwhile, however, there remains reason in Quiggin's conclusion,[28] reached after an investigation of the late bardic verse: "The political decay which was caused by the storm and stress of the Viking invasions is only too clearly reflected in the literature of the centuries after the death of Brian Boruma. From about the beginning of the second millennium of our era onwards Ireland loses her high place among the literary peoples of Western Europe."

Whatever one's personal opinion of the general mass of lyric verse in Irish, Sigerson (not alone in many of his views) claimed for its authors vast originality and influence:[29] for instance, that they "introduced rime into European literature" and refined it exquisitely; invented "broken staves" (mingling short with long lines); produced the first nature verse and sea songs; influenced Latin literature (as shown by Latin hymns cast in "Gaelic forms") and the literatures deriving therefrom, as well as the Germanic (one of St. Gall's pupils having "introduced rime into German"); initiated "bilingual song" (mingling Gaelic and Latin) in the Hymn of St. Colman (†661); produced in *A Vision of Viands* "the earliest . . . mock-heroic poem in (non-classic) European literature"; and originated, in *rosg*, blank verse, though herein all lines

---

28 *Op. cit.,* 90.
29 See intro., *op. cit.,* p. 2 *et passim.*

open with the same word, exemplifying deliberate initial identical rhyme. The same enthusiast feels that Irish poets had already achieved great diversity of verse form in the possibly pre-Christian "Cuchulainn Period," with "internal or inlaid rime," the burden (in Cuchulainn's lament for Ferdiad), double end (and internal) rhyme, etc.

In connection with these latter considerations, it should be emphasized that old Irish verse was technically often very complicated in design. The earliest extant specimens (sixth century), unrhymed but not unalliterative, were succeeded by pieces illustrative of a metrical system rooted in syllable-counting and consonantal rhyme and favoring intricate patterns that emphasized short-lined quatrains, with enjambment between second and third lines prohibited and each stanza fully self-contained in idea. Hyde[30] has explained how in this system the poets "divided the consonants into *groups,* and any consonant belonging to a particular group was allowed to rhyme with any other consonant belonging to the same. Thus a word ending in *t* could rhyme with a word ending in *p* or *c*, but with no other. . . ." The same historian provides the following "classification":[31]

S stood by itself . . .
P.C.T. called soft consonants [really hard not soft].
B.G.D. called hard consonants [. . . rather soft than hard].
F. [Ph.] CH. TH. called rough consonants.
LL. M. NN. NG. RR. called strong consonants.
Bh. Dh. Ch. [*sic*: misprint for Gh.] Mh. L.N.R. called light consonants.

The metrical system just considered began to suffer

---

[30] *Literary History* . . . , cit., 539–40.
[31] *Ibid.,* 540, fn.—Miss Hull (*Text-Book* . . . , *cit.,* I, 224, fn.) adds *sh* to the fourth category.

change in the seventeenth century, probably as one result of the break-up of the Bardic Schools, which had preserved old traditions in a system of metrical rules drawn from codifications that go back to pre-ninth-century treatises; vowel rhyme replaced consonantal, stress supplanted syllable-counting as a governing factor, and short lines yielded to long. Nevertheless, structure—with internal assonance—remained fairly complicated, to say the least, for among other subtleties the Irish found rhyme-correspondence between the heavy vowels (*o, u,* and *a*) and between the light (*i* and *e*).

C. Bronze: The Major Story Cycles[32]

The majority of early Irish tales which have counted most for later times—and most clearly nourished the imagination of post-Victorian "Renaissance" authors—may be arbitrarily apportioned among fairly well-defined cycles. It is common to speak of four—sometimes five—such cycles: the Mythological, the Historical, the Ulster (or Red Branch), the Fenian, and (very loosely conceived of) the Post-Fenian. Comment on the miscellaneous matter of the last is here omitted; the Mythological and so-called "Historical" tales (the latter of which—some seventy—may be grouped in sub-cycles concerned with various kings) are considered in one section, being sometimes only debatably separable, though indeed the "Historical" are also sometimes questionably distinguishable from the Ulster and Fenian, since—as Professor Dillon confesses[33]—"the boundary between legend and history

---

[32] Usefully to be consulted would be the series "The Old Irish Bardic Tales," by R. I. B[est], in *The United Irishman,* 10 Oct. 1902–25 Apr. 1903.

[33] *Cycles of the Kings, cit.,* 2.

cannot be fixed." What follows is intended as a brief general account of the three main groupings indicated, with recollection of the essential themes of illustrative stories associated with them (stories which sometimes exist in variant forms).

1. Mythological Cycle and "Historical" Tales

The material of the Mythological Cycle is, as Hyde records,[34] mostly "to be found only in brief digests preserved in the Leabhar Gabhála, or Book of Invasions of Ireland, of which large fragments exist in the Books of Leinster and Ballymote, and which Michael O'Clery (collecting from all the ancient sources which he could find in his day) rewrote about the year 1630."[35] This work, at times suggestive of epic quality, is a curious mixture of tradition, historical fiction, and history. Of course its essential theme is the general legendary history of Ireland, but its actual concern is largely with the coming—and battles—of the Milesians; this is to say that its heroes are pagan gods and its concentration is on the pre-Christian era. On it, the seventeenth-century Geoffrey Keating based the initial portion of his history of Ireland, *Foras Feasa ar Éirinn.*

We are told how (aside from the unfortunate Cessair and her company: *v.* II, *sup.*) Parthalón, of Japhet's line, leads the first settlement of 5000, three centuries after the Biblical Flood, though fated eventually to die of plague with all his people except one man.[36] Nemed appears next (within thirty years) with an expedition from

---

[34] *Literary History . . . , cit.,* 281.
[35] Cf. *Lebor Gabála Érenn,* ed. and trans. R. A. S. Macalister. 5 v. Dublin: Irish Texts Soc'y, 1938–56.
[36] Tuan mac Cairill, grandson of his brother Sera: cf. James Stephens, *Irish Fairy Tales.*

Scythia. The Nemedians fight the oppressive Fomorians successfully until Nemed himself dies of plague, after which the Fomorians, supposedly the monstrous progeny of Ham, proceed to collect a yearly tribute of two-thirds of the Nemedian children, cattle, and corn until desperation stimulates further fighting—and the eventual departure from Ireland of most of the remaining Nemedians after their defeat at Conand's Tower (*Tor Conaind*). Those departing divide into three groups: one goes to Greece—and slavery; one to northern Europe; one—headed by Briton Mael—to Scotland, where their descendants are eventually overcome by the Picts. After two centuries the descendants of the Greek Nemedians return to Ireland, under five leaders, as the "Firbolg," or "men of the bags," so named because—unless O'Rahilly (*Early Irish History and Mythology*, 52-53) is correct in translating their name as "Men of the god Bolg" (god of lightning; cf. I-E. *bheleg*: "flash")—during their period in Greece they were forced to labor at carrying soil in bags (*builg*) from the valleys to elevated places for covering rock.[37] They possess the country peacefully for about thirty-five years—until they are overcome at the first battle of Moytura by the Tuatha Dé Danann, reputed to have come to Ireland in a "magic mist" but themselves descendants of the band of Nemedians who had emigrated to northern Europe! Approximately two centuries later the Milesians appear—and fight their way to sovereignty over the Tuatha Dé Danann, who mostly retire underground as *síde* (elf-folk), their supplanters ruling until in turn conquered by the English.

---

[37] Or because they carried bags of Irish clay to Greece as protection against serpents, or used these bags later in building ships for their invasion. They are also known as *Fir Domnann* and *Gáilióin*.

The Mythological tales, which, in Joyce's phrase,[38] are "less numerous and less consecutive" than those of the cycles still to be discussed, are sometimes thought to be related—with the older tales in the Welsh *Mabinogion,* which adapt or parallel the names of some of the Irish divinities (cf., *e.g.,* Ir. *Danu,* Welsh *Dôn;* Ir. *Manannan,* W. *Manawydan;* etc.—and cp. Rees, *op. cit.*)—to a vast body of lost material. Important examples would be *The Second Battle of Moytura, The Courtship of Etain, The Story of Baile . . . , The Fate of the Children of Tuireann,* and *The Fate of the Children of Ler*—the last two constituting with the Deirdre story from the Ulster Cycle the "Three Sorrows of Story-Telling."

Of the tales mentioned, *The Second Battle of Moytura* (*Mag Tuired:* "Pillared Plain")[39] is, at least in casual reference, likely to cause some confusion because it really involves accounts of two battles. The first battle,[40] at Southern Moytura (near modern Cong, County Mayo), is fought by the Tuatha Dé Danann under Nuada against the Firbolg under Eochaid. After four days the latter are routed, but Nuada loses a hand—and therefore, being blemished, the kingship, which is bestowed on Breas ("Handsome"), son of Eiriu by a Fomorian king, on the understanding that he will resign if unsatisfactory. Meanwhile, according to some versions of the *Lebor Gabála,* some of the routed Firbolg escape to Aran (where tremendous fortifications remain), the Hebrides, and else-

---

[38] *Social History . . . , cit.,* I, 536.—For some lovely retellings, see Ella Young's *Celtic Wonder Tales.*—Cf. A. Furlong, "The Influence of the Literature of Ancient Ireland on 'The Mabinogion,'" *Irish Packet,* X, 250 (11 July 1908), 425–27.

[39] See W. Stokes, "The Second Battle of Moytura," *Revue Celtique,* XII, 52–130, for text and trans. of MS. Harleian 5280 (British Museum).— Summary in fragmentary *Lebor Gabála* prefix, *Book of Leinster.*—Cf. Best, *United Irishman,* 14 Feb. 1903.

[40] For text and tr. see J. Fraser, *Ériu,* VIII, 1.

where; and the Fomorians proceed to make the Tuatha
Dé Danann generally miserable.

Breas proves wholly unsatisfactory (incidentally,
Coirpre, a poet he slights, utters the initial Irish satire!)
and the Tuatha Dé Danann demand his abdication; he
accedes, but—having gained by request a seven-year respite—goes treacherously for aid to the Fomorians, en-
listing that of Balor,[41] King of the Isles of Norway (in
O'Rahilly's view a Celtic sun-god), where a great army is
gathered. Meanwhile Nuada, having got a movable silver
hand from Diancecht, resumes the kingship and is joined
by Lugh (actually Balor's grandson). After a year of
secret pondering by Lugh and his fellows, alliances are
contracted and preparations to fight the Fomorians, covering some years, are made. Eventually the second battle of
Moytura (really Northern Moytura, modern Moytirra,
Sligo) takes place. There is great fighting: Balor—he of
the devastatingly poisonous single eye—slays Nuada;
Lugh slays Balor; Breas is captured, but spared when the
Fomorians flee; and the Dagda, Nuada's successor as
king, recovers his famous harp.—Very late accounts,
which yet seem to incorporate some early material, it may
be added, speak of a *third* battle of Moytura, fought in
Galway.

The Courtship of Etain,[42] chief of a group of three

---

41 For whom, incidentally, Ella Young invents a son in her delightful
Unicorn with Silver Shoes.—Murphy sees in the opposition of Fomorians
and Tuatha Dé a parallel to that of the Greek Titans and Olympian gods
(*Saga and Myth in Ancient Ireland,* 18–19).
42 *Tochmarc Étaine,* ed. and trans. O. Bergin and R. I. Best (Dublin,
1938). Partially preserved in the *Book of the Dun Cow,* the full text (a
segment of the *Yellow Book of Lecan*), printed in *Ériu* XII, is in the
National Library of Ireland and is summarized by Dillon in *Irish Sagas,*
20–26. James Stephens' *In the Land of Youth* includes an incomparably
beautiful version of this story, to which W. B. Yeats's *The Two Kings* also
relates.—Cf. also "Fiona Macleod's" *The Immortal Hour,* Ella Young's
The Golden Fly, Standish O'Grady's "The Secret Bride," *History of Ire-*

overlapping tales, conjecturally dated from about the time of the Ulster Cycle, needs—despite its essential loveliness —no detailed outlining here, as its fundamental concern has already been indicated in the identification of Etain's original husband, the minor divinity Midir.

The Story of Baile . . . ,[43] classified among the "king stories" by Dillon and often regarded as "charming," though in the writer's opinion extravagantly absurd, tells of the lovers Baile Mac Buain and Aillinn, daughter of Lughaidh, and of how they died grieving at false news (given—apparently gratuitously!—by a specter) of each other's death. From Baile's grave grows a yew bearing at its top a likeness of the dead lover's head; from Aillinn's grave, a similarly decorated apple. Seven years later the trees are cut down, and on tablets made from their wood is inscribed a record of the visions, espousals, loves, and courtships of Ulster and Leinster. Later, when Art, son of Conn of the Hundred Battles, is holding these tablets, they leap together, never to be disunited, though fated to be lost in the burning of Tara.[44]

The Fate of the Children of Tuireann,[45] in extant form thought to be of late manuscript-derivation (though Thurneysen has recalled—*Zeitschrift für celtische Philologie*, XII, 239—a much earlier version), is, after a loosely related introduction dealing with Nuada and the

---

land: *Heroic Period*, James H. Cousins' *Etain the Beloved* (Dublin, 1912), Padraic Colum's *The King of Ireland's Son*, and Yeats's "The Harp of Aengus," prefatory to *The Shadow Waters.*—Cf. further O'Curry, Lect. 9, *Manners and Customs, cit.*

[43] Trans. K. Meyer, *Revue Celtique*, XIII (1892) ; oldest (? 11th century) recension in MS. Harleian 5280.

[44] W. B. Yeats utilized this story in *Baile and Aillinn*. See also his "Ribh at the Tomb of Baile and Aillinn" (*Supernatural Songs*).

[45] R. I. A. MSS. 23.G.10, 23.E.16, 23.M.47 (imperfect) ; early reference in *Cormac's Glossary;* ed. and tr. R. J. O'Duffy (Dublin, 1901) ; also tr. Joyce, *Old Celtic Romances*. See Cross-Slover, *Ancient Irish Tales*.

troublesome Fomorians, in its main theme the story of the difficulties of Tuireann's sons—Brian, Iuchar, and Iucharba,[46] brothers of Ethne—in meeting Lugh's heavy and miscellaneous stipulations for *eric* (including apples from the garden of the Hesperides as the first—and not the most difficult!) after they have slain his father, Cian: difficulties so great that by the time Lugh's exactions have been satisfied, death alone remains, since the god vengefully refuses succor. In consequence, Tuireann himself makes an elegy and dies on the bodies of his sons, with whom he is buried.

The Fate of the Children of Ler,[47] apparently ancient only in theme, some of its incidents having parallels in early Irish story and interspersed songs being seemingly older than their prose setting, is a sad and moving tale in which Ler, ordinarily the old sea god, is a Dé Danann king living in a *sid* in northern Ireland after the Milesian victory at Taillte. Their originally loving stepmother (Ler's third wife), jealous of the fatherly affection, transforms his four children (three sons and a daughter) by a druidic wand into swans, doomed thereafter to nine hundred years of suffering (on Lake Darvra—now Derryveragh, Westmeath; on the "Moyle," between Scotland and Ireland; and on the ocean west of Galway and Mayo), while she herself is in punishment changed into a "demon of the air"

---

[46] In Eleanor Hull's opinion (*Text-Book . . . , cit.,* I, 87) "probably originally one," but in any case "doublets of the Tuatha Dé Danann kings, Mac Cuill, Mac Cecht, and Mac Greine."

[47] Eighteenth-century MSS.: R. I. A. 23.C.26; Univ. College Dublin (Mac Curtin); Trinity College Dublin (O'Daly); British Museum (Tipper). Trans. by O'Curry (*Atlantis,* Nos. vii–viii), Joyce (*Old Celtic Romances*), R. J. O'Duffy (Dublin, 1883).—Katharine Tynan's "The Story of Aibhric" (*Shamrocks:* London, 1887) is based on this; John Todhunter included this and the "Turann" story in *The Banshee and Other Poems* (1888). One may also cf. George Sigerson's verse *Saga of King Ler* (c. 1913).

by her foster father, Bodb Derg. The spell over, the swans return to find Ler's *síd* empty and desolate. St. Kemoc seeks them out and, after their transformation into wizened old people, baptizes them at their urgent request—after which they immediately die, to be buried standing together, as desired.

As examples of the more clearly historical tales[48] may be particularized *The Destruction of Dinn Ríg, The Destruction of Da Derga's Hostel, The Adventures of the Sons of Eochu Muigmedón, Bórama,* and *The Wooing of Becfola.* Of these, *The Destruction of Dinn Ríg,*[49] for centuries regarded as first of the Irish "king stories," is in subject matter a dreadful affair about what ensued as a result of the murder of King Loegaire and his son by the former's jealous brother Cobthach. After the murders, Cobthach seizes Leinster and banishes his brother's grandson, Labhraidh Moen.[50] The latter shortly marries Moriath, princess of Fir Morca, and her father undertakes to help Labhraidh regain his kingdom. The resultant attack on Dinn Ríg succeeds after Labhraidh's harper incapacitates the defenders by playing the famous sleep-strain, and Labhraidh becomes ruler of Leinster. Then, in an extension of the original tale, he takes his revenge by literally roasting Cobthach and hundreds of the latter's company to death in a guesthouse secretly built of iron after Cobthach has accepted an invitation to visit.

The Destruction of Da Derga's Hostel, which may be found in almost complete form in *The Book of the Dun*

[48] See Dillon, *The Cycles of the Kings, cit.*
[49] Portion of *Longes Labrada* ("Voyage of Labraid"). In *Book of Leinster, Yellow Book of Lecan,* and Rawlinson MS. B.502; trans. W. Stokes, *Zeitschrift für celtische Philologie,* III.—Cf. Keating's history and O'Curry's *Manuscript Materials* and *Manners and Customs.*
[50] Cf. the author's *Carved in Findruine* and Padraic Colum's *The Story of Lowry Maen.*—The hero's name means "The dumb speaks."

Cow (one of eight manuscripts),[51] is thought since its original appearance (perhaps prior to the eighth century) to have made accretions, including part of the *Courtship of Etain* story, Conaire's fate apparently having been decided by the anger of the *síde* over his grandfather's having wed Midir's wife and later destroyed Bri-Leith (Midir's mound) in attempting to recover her after Midir's repossession, though his own evil foster brothers are the agents of destruction. Indeed, the story begins with a description of Etain. Hyde, confessing inability to do more than guess at the translation of much of it, calls it,[52] "after the Táin Bo Chuailgne, probably the oldest and most important saga in the whole range of Irish literature."

Conaire, elected king, has to banish his wicked foster brothers, among others, whereupon they become pirates, joining strength with another—Prince Ingcel, banished for wickedness by his own father, the King of Britain. The *síde* cause Conaire to break his *geasa,* insuring trouble. En route from Clare to Tara, the king finds Meath in flames from the marauding of the pirates; so he turns aside into Da Derga's ("Red's") Hostel, situated in the hills near Dublin, and straddling the river Dodder. The watching foster brothers beach their ships south of the Liffey and send a spy to reconnoiter. Then follows a wildly colorful report to the pirates on the guests of the Hostel—their identification, capacities, and prophesied performances as members of Conaire's company: all this through utilization of the Homeric question-and-answer device. Eventually the pirates cross the Dublin Mountains and fire the

---

[51] Version with trans. by Stokes, *Revue Celtique,* XX.
[52] *Literary History . . . , cit.,* 388; cf. Thurneysen, *Die Irische Helden- und Königsage.*—Padraic Colum's *The Destruction of the Hostel* relates to this story.

house; Conaire and his men emerge to fight furiously, but finally a wizard thirst is placed on the king to incapacitate him, with the result that he and most of his company are finally butchered. Conaire's head is being struck off by two pirates just as his marvelous champion Mac Cecht is returning from a desperate but finally successful search for water: when Mac Cecht pours the water into Conaire's gullet, the head revives to praise his valor and regret the dead king's inability to reward him! Mac Cecht himself and Conall Cearnach, though both are badly wounded, survive the general carnage. The imagination of the Celt has seldom shaken more fiery locks than in this thundering saga.

The Adventures of the Sons of Eochu Muigmedón[53] traces the story of how Niall of the Nine Hostages became King of Ireland. King Eochu had four sons by Mongfind, his first wife, and one—Niall—by his second, the Saxon princess Cairenn Chasdub, who was hated and treated as a menial by Mongfind. Niall, born out-of-doors while his mother was carrying water, was rescued and reared by the poet Torna, who saw him to kingly age and then brought him to Tara, where the prophet-smith Sithchenn confirmed his preëminence over his half-brothers. Lost on a hunting trip later, the five boys are thirsty and seek water. A well is found, guarded by an indescribably horrible hag—the "loathly lady" of tradition (cf. the later English *Wedding of Sir Gawain and Dame Ragnell* and its analogues)—who demands a kiss in exchange for water. The sons of Mongfind refuse, one by one; Niall both kisses and lies with her—only to have her change into a

---

[53] See W. Stokes edn. and trans., *Revue Celtique*, XXIV; cf. *Silva Gadelica*, I, 328 and II, 370; cf. Saul, *Carved in Findruine*.

marvelously beautiful woman who reveals herself as "Sovereignty" and predicts his succession (later confirmed) to Eochu.

Bórama (*Book of Leinster*)[54] is a highly episodic tale rooted, as Hyde recognized, in a Procne-Philomela situation. Tuathal, King of Ireland (76-106), has two daughters—the elder Fithir, the younger Dáirine. Eochu, King of Leinster, comes a-wooing and, in accordance with Irish custom, gets Fithir to wife. His subjects counting Dáirine preferable, he announces that Fithir is dead (though really only concealed); thus he wins Dáirine. When Fithir sees Dáirine, she dies of shame, whereupon Dáirine dies of sorrow. (Cailte recalls the story in the *Colloquy of the Ancients, q.v. inf.*) Having learned the truth, Tuathal, with the kings of Connacht and Ulster as allies, conquers Leinster. Eochu is slain, but his son Erc is permitted to succeed him, although an *eric* in the form of a tremendous annual tribute is laid upon Leinster. The tale then gives the history of how this exaction was collected, resisted, and collected off and on through the centuries until St. Molling —really by verbal trickery—in 674 finally obtained its remission from Finnachta, then King of Ireland. Several episodes concern battles fought to win payment; and one of these, the Battle of Dún Bolg (594), really constitutes the major part of the story.

In *The Wooing of Becfola*,[55] a woman comes to Diarmuid, King of Tara (and son of Aed Slane, High King during the early part of the seventh century); he takes her, giving her as bride-price a little brooch—wherefore

---

54 Cf. *Revue Celtique*, XIII.
55 See *Silva Gadelica*, I, 85; II, 91.—Cf. James Stephens, *Irish Fairy Tales*.

a druid names her *Bec* [Mod. Ir. *Beg*] *Fola* ("Small Dowry"). Becfola promptly makes unsuccessful attempts to seduce Crimthann (son of Aed of Leinster), Diarmuid's fosterling, Crimthann's people preventing when he finally agrees to a sunrise assignation: hoping to meet him, she leaves her husband's bed early one Sunday morning and goes with a maid into Leinster; unwittingly led into faery, she chances to meet the young warrior Flann O'Fedach, with whom she sleeps (though—quite against her desire—untouched) on Dam Inis ("Ox Island," Loch Erne), for which he and three relatives are contending against another quartet of warriors. Later Becfola returns to Diarmuid (unaware—as a mortal living in *mortal time* —of her absence), remaining until Flann, a year later, comes for her as the wounded but only survivor of the island contention and takes her away with him.

The Death of Mael Fothartaig, Son of Rónán,[56] though without any historical basis, may also be here recalled, merely for its barbaric beauty. Herein the widower Rónán, King of Leinster, marries the young daughter of Eochaid, King of Dunseverick, against the advice of his handsome son, Mael Fothartaig. The queen variously solicits her upright stepson's love; disappointed, she charges such solicitation on the part of the prince in collusion with a foster brother named Congal, and Rónán promptly has both boys slain, though they reveal the truth before they die by the spear of Aedán. Dond, Congal's brother, later beheads the queen's parents and brother, throwing their heads at her. She stabs herself, and Rónán dies lamenting after

---

[56] Title Dillon's rendering of *Fingal Rónáin* in *Early Irish Literature, q.v. The Book of Leinster* contains one of two extant versions.—Cf. Saul, *Carved in Findruine.*

Mael's sons have killed Aedán.—This story,[57] older than
the twelfth-century manuscript which preserves it, recalls,
as Kuno Meyer noted, the old Greek tale of Hippolytus, a
youth also tragically unresponsive to the advances of his
stepmother (Phaedra).

As a pendant to the group of tales just recalled, may
here be outlined *The Adventure of Art, Son of Conn,*[58] in
which the experiences of the historical characters are entirely referable to contact with mythological figures.

Conn, lamenting at Ben Etair maic Etgaith the death of
his wife, Ethne Taebfada, sees a lovely girl approaching
in a coracle. Though pretending to be Delbchaem ("Fair
Shape"), daughter of King Morgan of the Land of Wonders, she is really Becuma Cneisgel, banished by the Dé
Danann because of unfaithfulness to her husband and now
confessedly seeking Art. However, she takes up with Conn
freely, binding him against his will to dismiss Art from
Tara for a year. On Art's banishment, the supply of corn
and milk fails; consulted druids blame the failure on Becuma's evil, saying the only remedy is to slay "the son of
a sinless couple" and mix his blood with the soil of Tara.
Conn, placing the rule in Art's hands, goes seeking such a
boy.

Entering a coracle found at Ben Etair, he is drifted to
a marvelous island, where he is well received by King
Daire Degamra and Queen Rigru Rosclethan, parents of
the boy Segda Saerlabraid. His request to take Segda to be
"bathed in the water of Ireland" to work that country's

---

[57] Greene (*Irish Sagas* ed. Dillon, 163) compares T. C. Murray's *Autumn
Fire.*—In one version, Dond slays Aedán.
[58] Cf. Stephens, "Becuma of the White Skin," *Irish Fairy Tales.*—The
only extant version of the original story is in the *Book of Fermoy:* see
Dillon, *Early Irish Literature,* for extended summary.

deliverance is refused, Daire explaining that he and his
queen (following their parents' example) had united only
at the child's "making"; when Segda insists on going, his
parents invoke the protection of the Irish kings, of Art,
and of Finn Mac Cumhall. When Conn's druids want later
to slay Segda, a woman, wailing behind a lowing cow, approaches. The challenged druids cannot tell the contents of
the bags carried by the cow (one on each side); the woman
tells them to slay the cow, mix its blood with the soil, and
then cut the bags to release a one-legged and a twelve-
legged bird. The released birds fight, the former (symbolizing the child) prevailing over the latter (symbolizing
the Irish). Then the boy and the woman (really Queen
Rigru) depart, the latter advising that the druids be
hanged and telling Conn to put away Becuma (whose
identity she reveals), under penalty of having Ireland
lose a third of its corn, milk, and mast while she remains.

Becuma next forces Art to play chess by threatening a
geis. He wins the first game—and makes it her penalty to
get Curoi Mac Dairi's wand before again eating in Ireland. She does so—and brings along 150 men of the fairy
folk, who help her win the next game. Thus Art is bound
to find Delbchaem on some unknown island. Voyaging in
another conveniently found coracle, he comes first to an
isle of women, where he stays with Creide Firalainn
("Truly Beautiful") a month and a half; she both foretells the nightmarish experiences to befall him in gaining
Delbchaem and gives him helpful advice. After terrific
later fighting, involving the slaying of her parents, Art
wins Delbchaem and the two go to Ireland, where Delbchaem sends Art ahead alone to order Becuma out of Tara.
The latter leaves wailing, and Art and Delbchaem are
happily received.

2. Ulster, or Red Branch, Cycle

What are generally called the "Red Branch" tales[59] (though it has been suggested that "Royal Branch" might be a more accurate designation) represent the heroic tradition of Uladh, or Eastern Ulster, comprising the modern Belfast area (roughly Counties Louth and Down), whose capital was Emain Macha ("The Twins of Macha"). The remains of Emain, referred to as the "Navan Fort," may still be seen several miles to the southwest of Armagh, Emain itself having supposedly been destroyed in A.D. 332. In the early days, it should be remembered, Ulster extended to the Boyne.

The tales in question are obviously so old as to have only an obscure and conjectural historical basis, if any at all: de Blacam, for example, appears to relate them to a cattle raid of the second century of the pre-Christian era; O'Rahilly (*Early Irish History and Mythology,* 271) assigns to them a purely mythological origin. It has been argued that they must have originated prior to the formation of Meath as a distinct province, since Meath receives no mention in them; and there are suggestive implications in Rhys's view of Cuchulainn as originally a Celtic sun-god—a view shared by many others, including Nutt and Loomis,[60] who sees this warrior (by virtue of Welsh transmigration) eventually transformed into the Arthurian Gawain. Watson, reviewing (and demolishing)[61] Ridgeway's "The Date of the First Shaping of the Cuchulainn Saga" (*Proceedings of the British Academy,* Vol. II), refers the tales to a period beyond 750 B.C.; and cer-

---

[59] See in general Thurneysen, *Die Irische Helden- und Königsage, cit.,* and Eleanor Hull, *The Cuchullin Saga in Irish Literature* (London, 1898).
[60] R. S. Loomis, *Celtic Myth and Arthurian Romance* (New York, 1926), 51 ff.
[61] *Celtic Review,* 15 Jan. 1908, 283 ff.

tainly the often-noted Homeric parallels (recalling the chariot-fighting with bronze weapons and broadly equating Cuchulainn with Achilles, Concobar with Agamemnon, Deirdre and Naoise with Helen and Paris) seem not without significance. And after all, there may be nothing but the shadow of monastic scribes in the preserved picture of Concobar (named for a river), or Conor, Mac Nessa (the king whom the Red Branch heroes serve, and the king to whose capital companies of warriors came each summer for drill and training) as one born in the hour of Christ's birth and destined to die of grief and fury on hearing of the Saviour's crucifixion. In any event, it would appear to be a moderate view to regard these tales as transmitted orally from early in the Christian era, probably first written down by Christian monks in the seventh or eighth century, and eventually incorporated in manuscripts dating from the eleventh to the fifteenth century—these late manuscripts being the source of our own knowledge of them.

As long recognized, the stories themselves, often broadly humorous and not lacking in admirable characterization, reflect an "aristocratic and war-like" temper subject to a surprisingly noble chivalric code. The chief leaders and heroes involved, beside Concobar, are the demigod Cuchulainn[62] (the greatest hero in Irish saga), Conall Cearnach ("the Victorious"), Loegaire the Triumphant, Celtchar of the Battles, Fergus ("Manly Strength") Mac Roy (Concobar's stepfather), the poet Bricriu of the Poison Tongue, Cathbad the Druid, Sencha Mac Ailill (the "wise old counsellor"), and the three sons of Usna—Naoise, Ainnle, and Ardan; with these should be men-

---

[62] One may cf. James H. Cousins, *The Hound of Uladh* (Adyar, Madras, Kalakshetra, 1946) ; Yeats's Cuchulainn plays; etc.

tioned Queen Medb of Connacht and her daughter (Fin-nabair), and Deirdre "of the Sorrows."—The Red Branch heroes, one may add here, used chariots in sports as well as in fighting and built many "duns," or forts.

Actually, the Ulster Cycle comprises more than a hundred highly miscellaneous tales, but the heart of the unorganized series is, of course, the group which makes up the greatest of Irish epics—the *Táin Bó Cuálnge*[63] ("Cattle-Raid of Cooley"), detailing a fantastic campaign which took place along the southern edge of Uladh. The basic texts of the *Táin*[64] are to be found in the *Book of the Dun Cow* and the *Book of Leinster* (whose version has been described as the more "literary" in character), though the later *Yellow Book of Lecan* contains an imperfect version which perhaps nevertheless represents the earliest of these three recensions.

The *Táin,* then, represents the central epic, though there is a group of shorter tales, or *remscéla* (the *Book of Leinster* lists ten[65]), leading up to it, as well as a group largely, but by no means exclusively, concerned with events subsequent to its episodes. The bulk of the entire cycle has been estimated by Alfred Nutt[66] as great enough to fill about two thousand printed octavo pages.

—And now to glance at the themes of representative tales, beginning with selections from the introductory group.

The Revealing of the Táin, presumably a late account, included in a satire called "Proceedings of the Great Bar-

---

[63] Named after a son of Breoghan, reputedly one of the Milesian invaders and father also of Muirthemne; Cúalnge is said to have been slain during the invasion. Cf. Keating's history, II, 81 and 97.
[64] On MSS., cf. Dillon, *Early Irish Literature,* 3–4.
[65] Cf. Thurneysen, *Die Irische Helden- und Königsage,* 248 ff.
[66] *Cuchulainn . . . , cit.,* 2.

dic Institution," says the story of the *Táin* had been lost by the seventh century—even from the recollection of the leading poets, assembled by Senchán Torpeist, Chief Poet of Erin. Inasmuch as it is known to be contained in "the Cuilmenn," a book supposedly carried off to the Continent, two poets are deputed to seek it. They first visit the tomb of Fergus Mac Roy, in Connacht, whereupon the old warrior's spirit appears and, over a three-day period, tells them the tale.—A recension of the essential story summarized by Professor Dillon in *The Cycles of the Kings* as "The Great Visitation to Guaire" makes the "saints of Ireland" the agents of recovery at the grave of Fergus.

The Debility of the Ultonians[67] explains the situation at the beginning of the *Táin*. It appears that Macha, a goddess, having suffered at Concobar's hands, had laid a curse on Ulster to the effect that when it was endangered, its king and his army would be prostrated by a weakness similar to that of women in childbed, leaving them unable to defend it. Hence, during Medb's raid only Cuchulainn, as a demigod exempt from the curse, was able to defend Uladh: he did so single-handed throughout that winter of war (except for three days and nights of supernatural relief, permitting him to sleep)!

The Birth of Cuchulainn: This title may serve to cover various accounts of the demigod's birth. All of them call Cuchulainn the son of Dechtire, Concobar's sister; the disagreement has to do with his paternity, which in certain somewhat suspect accounts is assigned to Sualtam, an Ulster chief. A seemingly older group of stories says Dechtire lay incestuously with Concobar, while others claim she was pregnant by the sun-god Lugh. (In one tale Lugh changes himself into an insect, hides in Dechtire's

---

[67] Cf. O'Connor, III, B, Fn. 32, above.

drinking vessel, and is swallowed, causing pregnancy; then he is reborn in the form of Cuchulainn.)

The *Táin Bó Regamna* is a wild tale telling how the Mórrigu, a war goddess, comes before the beginning of Medb's raid to warn Cuchulainn of a short life and give notice that she means to try to slay him. The tale is connected with other material, including that known as "The Adventures of Nera,"[68] for an incomparable revitalization of which one should see James Stephens' *In the Land of Youth,* the more particularly because the manuscript material recording Nera's wild experiences tying a withe on the foot of a hanged man at Samhain, and his incursions into the fairy mound at Cruachan, is confused in character.

Passing by such *remscéla* as those dealing with Medb's cattle raids to provide for her expedition, we may next recall *The Dispute of the Swineherds,* which is interesting partly for its illustration of the old Celtic belief in the transmigration of souls, or "doctrine of rebirth,"[69] but mainly as an explanation of the enmity of the two famous bulls involved in the *Táin.* It appears that the bulls had started their existence centuries before as swineherds to

---

[68] *Echtrai Nerai,* named in the *Book of Leinster,* is preserved untitled in MS. Egerton 1782, 71b–73b (British Museum; 15th century), and—as the *Tain Bo Aingin*—in the *Yellow Book of Lecan.* K. Meyer ed. and trans. the Egerton in *Revue Celtique,* X; a version by Lady Gregory may be found in her *Cuchulain of Muirthemne* (London & New York, 1902).

[69] See Nutt, fn. 1, III, A, above. Best ("Old Irish Bardic Tales," *United Irishman,* 28 Mar. 1903) amalgamates portions of Nutt's summary of the *Book of Leinster* version and Windisch's German translation of the MS. Egerton 1782 (British Museum) version to produce a readable one, "The Begetting of the Two Swineherds."—In Ella Young's words ["An Ancient Doctrine," *Irish Review,* No. 18 (Aug. 1912: really the sixth no. of Vol. II), p. 314], "The Celts believed that the soul came out of a beautiful and undying world to manifest itself here through the medium of a body and returned again to that world from whence it might emerge many times and take each time a new earth-body . . . the soul might go back to the divine world and converse with its comrades; this happened in vision or ecstasy, or when the body was in a deep trance . . ."

the gods and experienced thereafter successive transformations, "always," as Eleanor Hull writes,[70] "after a terrific struggle which shook . . . Ireland"; *e.g.*, they had been ravens—sea-beasts—champions—eventually worms which, on being swallowed, impregnated two cows, leading to the swineherds' rebirth as bulls.

The Fate of the Children of Usna[71] (one, it will be recalled, of the "Three Sorrows of Story-Telling") is detailed in many manuscripts, datable from the twelfth to the eighteenth century—perhaps later; and the different recensions offer many variations in detail. Originally a spare, barbaric tale, the essential story is still the loveliest and most moving in Irish literature—and quite possibly the finest of its kind in world literature. Retold many times in English,[72] it is recalled at this point because, although not always remembered as among them, it is logically one of the *remscéla,* since it explains the alliance between Fergus and Medb in the *Táin;* its oldest text appears to be

---

[70] *Text-Book . . . , cit.,* I, 38.—See James Stephens, "The Feast of Samhain," in *In the Land of Youth.*

[71] Cf. versions and editions by Geoffrey Keating (in his seventeenth-century history), T. O'Flanagan (1808), E. O'Curry (1862), E. Windisch (in *Irische Texte,* 1880), V. Hull (1949). Joyce has a translation in *Old Celtic Romances.*

[72] *E.g.,* by J. M. Synge, in *Deirdre of the Sorrows,* and by James Stephens, in *Deirdre*—two of the most remarkable versions. W. B. Yeats treated the end of the tragedy in his *Deirdre,* and there are versions by "Fiona Macleod," "A. E.," R. D. Joyce, Douglas Hyde, *et al.*—including the curious variant collected from oral tradition by Alexander Carmichael (see *Transactions of the Gaelic Soc'y of Inverness,* Vols. xiii and xiv), the one in the form of an opera libretto by Coulter, and the one constituting Part II of Terence Gray's *Cuchulainn / An Epic-Drama of the Gael*—a huge, dull affair in which Deirdre is pictured as a sulky, stubborn, selfish woman whose death is caused by an accidental fall from Concobar's chariot, while Naoise is hardly recognizable as the hero of tradition. One may also name Herbert Trench's *Deirdre Wedded* (1900) and Gordon Bottomley's *Deirdire* (1944). The present writer's *Felim's Daughter* (orig. in *Poet Lore,* LVIII, 4. 291–310) also retells the Deirdre tragedy; it is included in his *Hound and Unicorn* (Philadelphia, 1969).

that in the *Book of Leinster,* where it is entitled "The Exile of the Sons of Uisnech."

The saga begins with King Concobar feasting and drinking with his heroes at the house of his head storyteller, Felim, at which time the latter's wife gives birth to a daughter, named "Deirdre" ("The Troubler") by Cathbad the Druid, who prophesies she will be an agent of great woe to Ulster—whereupon the Ultonians want to slay her. Concobar prevents this, however, saying she is to be reared to be his future queen. Accordingly, she is brought up in a fortress of the Red Branch, supposedly seeing no one but her tutor and her nurse, Lavarcam. But despite close guard, she does see—and fall in love with—Naoise, whom she induces to carry her off to Alba (Scotland). With his brothers Ainnle and Ardan, the other sons of Usna, they escape—accompanied, according to one manuscript discovered by Hyde, by 150 warriors. Life is, on the whole, happy in Alba for some years; then Concobar's mischief begins. Having determined the sentiments of several warriors, he finds that only Fergus Mac Roy does not threaten personal reprisal should he injure the sons of Usna (his own nephews) ; therefore he sends Fergus (persuaded of his good intentions) and the latter's two sons to offer the fugitives peaceful return. In the end they win Naoise over, despite Deirdre's opposition and warning.

Concobar's treachery begins as soon as they reach Ireland: he has a certain Barach invite Fergus to a feast, knowing it is one of the latter's *geasa* to be unable to refuse such an invitation. Having thus separated Fergus from the exiles, Concobar next has them sent to the House of the Red Branch, instead of receiving them in his own mansion, where he is feasting. Late that night the drunken king sends Lavarcam to see whether Deirdre is still beautiful; out of her love, Lavarcam warns the lovers—and returns to tell Concobar Deirdre has lost her beauty. His jealousy temporarily eased, Concobar continues carousing —but later sends another retainer (whose father and brothers were slain by Naoise) to spy. Meanwhile Naoise and the others have locked and barred the Red Branch for defense. The spy, however, finds a top back window open, climbs up, and—peering in—has an eye torn out when Naoise hurls a chessman. The spy returns and tells Concobar his loss was justified by sight of so lovely a woman as Deirdre—whereupon Concobar begins his all-night assault on the Red Branch. Finally, Ilaun, one of Fergus' sons, is slain; and the other, Buine, is bought off with a bribe. At dawn Cathbad the Druid consents to take the others with a spell on Concobar's pledge not to injure the sons of Usna; thus it is that the brothers, escaping with Deirdre, think they are plunged into waves and, throwing down their weapons to swim, are easily taken. Concobar, breaking his word, has the boys promptly beheaded, whereupon Cathbad curses Emania and Concobar's house—the curse, incidentally, later working itself out in Medb's *táin*.

The story (which does not lack certain analogies in Sanskrit and elsewhere) has various conclusions. In what may be its eldest form, Concobar forces Deirdre to live with him for a year (Naoise herein having been slain immediately on reaching Emania) ; and then, angry at her suffering and rebuffs, proposes to turn her over for a year to Owen, the slayer of her husband—only to have her leap from the chariot in which the three are riding and dash her head on a rock—successfully. In other accounts, however, Deirdre utters her lament, either drinks of Naoise's blood or stabs herself, leaps into the grave of the three boys, and dies.

—Because of Concobar's treachery, Fergus then burns Emania and—with about fifteen hundred others of sympathetic mind—goes to Connacht to serve Oilioll and Medb, rulers there, and for some seven or ten years raid the Ultonians in revenge, ultimately joining Medb in the great *Táin*, which must next be reviewed.

The theme of the *Táin Bó Cuálnge*, most notable and extensive of Irish sagas, whose earliest redaction was dated the seventh century by Zimmer,[73] has been conveniently analyzed into eight divisions by Eleanor Hull, and I shall briefly summarize it with these general divisions in mind.

Part I may be called the "prologue." Herein we have a bedroom argument between King Oilioll (Ailill) and Queen Medb[74] (Meadhbh, Meve, etc.) of Connacht (whose exact ancient boundaries, by the way, are today indeterminable) as to which is the richer. Argument leads to anger—and decision to have all their property collected for comparison; this being done, they find themselves about equally wealthy except in one respect: a great bull, known as the *Finn-bheannach* ("White-horned"), originally calved by one of Medb's cows, had, scorning petticoat rule, gone over to Oilioll's herds. The restless queen

---

[73] See in general E. Windisch's edn. (*Die Altirische Heldensage . . . Táin Bó Cuálnge . . .* : Leipzig & London, 1905), extensively reviewed by Mackinnon in the *Celtic Review,* 15 July 1907, 88 ff.; *The Ancient Irish . . . Táin Bó Cúalnge,* tr. J. Dunn (London, 1914) ; E. Hull, *The Cuchullin Saga in Irish Literature* (London, 1898) ; Lady Gregory, *Cuchulain of Muirthemne, cit.*—The earliest preserved version, of perhaps ninth-century genesis, is in the *Book of the Dun Cow.*
[74] The name is "cognate with the Welsh *meddw,* 'drunk,' and related to the English word *mead.* She is 'the intoxicating one.'" (Rees, *Celtic Heritage,* 75.)

finds by inquiry that a certain Dare, of Cualnge, in Ulster, has a remarkable Dun Bull; so she sends an embassy seeking to borrow it for a year. Dare is courteous and obliging till one of the embassy gets drunk and says that if he had not given the bull they would have taken it—whereupon he dismisses the group angrily.[75] Medb promptly (in the second division of the saga) collects her armies, aided by Fergus Mac Roy and his vengeful Ulstermen, as well as by armies from Leinster and Munster. Then (having secretly promised her beautiful daughter, Finnabair, to various leaders to ensure vigorous allegiance) she leads her host across the Shannon at Athlone, finally pitching camp at Kells. Having reached the border of Ulster, however, the invaders are harassed by Cuchulainn, whereupon Medb asks about this—as it appears—seventeen-year-old hero. Fergus and a couple of other Ultonians tell her in detail, this material—comprising about a sixth of the entire saga—constituting the third division, known as the "Boy-Deeds of Cuchulainn"—in Frank O'Connor's view, an interpolation, as much else in the work may be.

It appears that Cuchulainn, whose name was originally "Setanta," was phenomenal even as a boy. For instance, he goes to Concobar's court at the age of five, routs the whole assembly of youth there, and has himself acknowledged chief; later, having slain the ferocious ban-dog of the smith Culann, he offers to assume its office until he has reared a substitute whelp, whereupon Cathbad the Druid names him "Cu Chulainn," or "Hound of Culann"; at the age of six he assumes arms—breaking every weapon offered him until he proves and accepts the king's own, smashing seventeen chariots before he finds one strong

---

[75] Austin Clarke, in *The Cattledrive in Connaught,* carries the story to this point. Cf. Saul, *Carved in Findruine.*

enough for his requirements. Thereafter he slays single-handed three notorious champions and on his return to court outruns and captures two stags; he approaches Emania still in his battle fury: "To overcome him, the ladies of the court appear before him unclad [or, as Standish J. O'Grady writes in *The Coming of Cuculain* (1894), "clad only in the pure raiment of their womanhood"!], and, when he shuts his eyes to the sight, he is seized, passed through three vats of cold water, which his fury causes to boil, and his rage departs from him."[76] —All this before the age of seven!—Little wonder that Fergus warns Medb of his potency. (One might add that, according to one saga, the poor fellow had plenty of *geasa* to observe, however: *e.g.,* it was *geis* to him to tell his "genealogy to one champion . . . to refuse combat to any one man, to look upon the exposed bosom of a woman, to come into a company without a second invitation, to accept the hospitality of virgins, to boast to a woman, to let the sun rise before him in Emania,"[77]etc.)

The fourth division comprises accounts of the long series of Cuchulainn's combats, culminating in the sad duel with Ferdiad ("The man of smoke"), whom he slays. Medb has requested an interview and tried to buy off this terrifying opponent—unsuccessfully; he has been killing a hundred men each night and will promise to desist only if Medb will consent—as she does—to keep her army in camp and send daily a warrior for single combat at the ford. A long succession of personal duels follows, including one in which the Mórrigu joins against the demigod. When Medb breaks her agreement and sends six men against him, Cuchulainn slays them all and resumes his night raids.

---

[76] Nutt, *Cuchulainn* . . . , *cit.,* 9.
[77] Hyde summary, *Literary History* . . . , *cit.,* 301.

Then, utterly worn out after a winter of single-handed fighting, the Ultonians still being helpless under their curse, he gets three days and nights of sleep to recuperate, his so-called *síde* father taking his place. He awakens furiously to accomplish what is known as the "Great Breach [or Rout] of Moy Muirthemne." This is followed by further combats until Medb forces his unwilling old friend Ferdiad to fight him. They fight three days, separating affectionately the first two nights; on the fourth day Cuchulainn finally kills Ferdiad with the *gae bulga,* a mysterious instrument usually floated down a stream and thrown from between the toes, though it could be used from above: "it made the wound of one spear in entering the body, but it had thirty barbs to open, and could not be drawn out of a person's body until it was cut open," according to one saga quoted by Hyde.[78] Cuchulainn himself has to be carried away for supernatural healing, however —and it is at this time that Medb's daughter, Finnabair,[79] really in love with an Ultonian, dies of a broken heart.

In the fifth division the Ulster warriors finally awaken to strength and the hosts begin to gather, Mac Roth, Medb's messenger, reporting somewhat in Homer's "catalogue of the ships" fashion, with Fergus identifying the Ultonians from the descriptions. (They include, incidentally, a notorious poet named Aithirne, of whom Fergus says, "The lakes and rivers recede before him when he satirises them, and rise up before him when he praises them."[80])

---

[78] *Ibid.,* 333. O'Rahilly (*op. cit.,* 58 ff.), however, regards it as a lightning-weapon of some sort; cf. R. S. Loomis, *Celtic Myth and Arthurian Romance* (New York, 1926), 48.

[79] Cf. Ella Young, *The Winning of Finovar* (orig. in *Sinn Féin,* 1 May 1909) ; also "Fionavar's Lover," *Nationality,* 17 Aug. 1918, p. 3, and *The Weird of Fionavar* (Dublin: Talbot Press, 1923).

[80] Hyde trans., *Literary History . . . , cit.,* 337.

The sixth section brings the great battle of Gairech and Ilgairech, during which the determined Medb sends the Dun Bull, surrounded by fifty heifers and eight men, to her Connacht palace, though the seventh division of the epic series finds her army completely routed and retreating to Cruachan, her seat in Connacht.

The eighth, and concluding, section details the battle of the two great bulls—which started as soon as they saw each other. They fought furiously all day—and during the succeeding night covered a large part of Ireland! "Next morning," in Hyde's graphic phraseology,[81] "the people of Cruachan saw the Dun Bull coming with the remains of his enemy upon his horns . . . The Dun made straight for his home . . . drank of the Shannon at Athlone, and . . . rushed . . . killing every one who crossed his way. Arrived there, he set his back to a hill and uttered wild bellowings of triumph, until 'his heart in his breast burst, and he poured his heart in black mountains of brown blood out across his mouth'."

Some half-dozen or so of a series of tales (aside from the *remscéla*) related or subsidiary to the *Táin* are of particular interest; these may be briefly recalled as follows:

The Battle of Rosnaree[82] concerns Concobar's angry humiliation at Medb's escape and capture of the Dun, or Brown, Bull, and his collection—on Cathbad's advice—of an army of mercenaries (not uncommon in ancient Ireland), with which he wars on the Kings of Leinster and Tara, Medb having declined to participate in the fighting. Cuchulainn saves the day for the nearly defeated Ulster-

---

[81] *Ibid.,* 340.
[82] Cf. Rev. E. Hogan, *The Battle of Rosnaree* (Todd Lect. Series, Vol IV, Royal Irish Academy, 1892), for trans.; Best, "Old Irish Bardic Tales" (*United Irishman,* 11 Apr. 1903), for summary of oldest (*Book of Leinster*) MS.

men and slays the King of Tara, whose son subsequently marries his daughter! This son, Erc, is in some tales named as the man who eventually cuts off Cuchulainn's head.

Various accounts of *Cuchulainn's Death*[83] survive. For convenience, I quote Nutt's summary of essentials, together with his reference to the related tale, *The Red Rout of Conall Cearnach* :[84]

"Three posthumous sons and three daughters are borne at one birth by the wife of the wizard Calatin.[85] These join with Lugaid, son of Curoi of Munster, with Erc, King of Tara, and with other chiefs whose fathers had been slain by Cuchulainn, and invade the hero's land. As he goes to his last fight he is begirt with terrible omens—the land is filled with smoke and flame, and weapons fall from their racks. His faithful charioteer refuses to harness his steed, the Grey of Macha [Cú's other chariot-horse, also a kelpie, or lake horse, was "the Black Sainglend"], and thrice does the horse turn his left side to his master. Then Cuchulainn reproaches him: he was not wont to deal thus with his master. So the Grey of Macha obeys, but as he does so, his big round tears of blood fall on Cuchulainn's feet. In vain do the thrice fifty queens who were in Emain Macha beseech him to stay. He turns his chariot from them, and they give a scream of wailing and lamentation, for they know he will not come to them again.

"As he fares onwards he encounters the three daughters of Calatin, as crones blind of the left eye. They are cook-

---

[83] The oldest version, in the *Book of Leinster,* is incomplete.

[84] *Cuchulainn* . . . , cit., 20–23.—See in general *The Death Tales of the Ulster Heroes,* ed. and trans. K. Meyer (Dublin, 1906) ; W. Stokes's summary, "Death of Cuchulinn," *Revue Celtique,* III, rptd. in Hull, *Cuchullin Saga* . . . , cit.

[85] Whom, with his twenty-seven other sons, Cú had slain in the great *Táin.*

ing a hound on a spit, and because Cuchulainn will not seem to scorn the offer of poor food, he accepts the flesh they present, although it was a *geis* . . . for him to do so. Then he comes in sight of his foes, and he rushes against them. 'The halves of their heads and skulls and hands and feet, and their red bones were scattered broadcast throughout the plain in numbers like unto the sand of the sea, and the stars of the heaven; like dewdrops in May; like leaves of the forest, and grass under the feet of the herbs [*sic*] on a summer's day. And grey was that field with their brains after the onslaught which Cuchulainn dealt out to them.'

"His spear is claimed of him. 'I need it myself,' says the hero. 'I will revile thee if thou givest it not,' says his foe. 'Never yet have I been reviled because of my niggardliness,' and with that Cuchulainn dashes his spear at the claimant, killing him and nine others. But with a cast of that spear Lugaid slays Laegh the charioteer. A second time the claim is made for the spear, and Cuchulainn is threatened that Ulster shall be reviled if he refuses. 'Never was Ulster reviled for my churlishness,' and again he parts with his weapon, and with it Erc, son of Ireland's high king, makes a cast that lights on the Grey of Macha, and he and Cuchulainn bid each other farewell. A third time the spear is claimed—Cuchulainn's kin should be defamed if he refuse. 'Tidings that my kin has been defamed shall never go back to the land to which I myself shall never return, for little of my life remains to me,' and again he parts with his weapon. Then Lugaid seizes it and strikes Cuchulainn, so that his bowels come forth on the cushions of the chariot, and the King of the Heroes of Erin is left dying alone on the plain. 'I would fain,' says he, 'go as far as that loch to drink a drink thereout.' 'We give thee leave if thou come again.' 'I will bid you come for me unless I return myself.' Then he gathers his bowels into his breast and drinks, and when he has drunk his eye rests upon a pillar stone in the plain; to it he fastens himself by his breast girdle, 'that he may not die seated nor lying down, but that he may die standing up.' His foes gather round him, but they dare not go to him, thinking him to be yet alive. But in vain does the Grey of Macha return to protect him, so long as his soul was in him, 'and fifty fall by his teeth and thirty by each of his hoofs.' Lugaid cuts off Cuchulainn's head, but even in death the hero avenges himself; the sword falls from his right hand and smites off that of Lugaid. They strike off Cuchulainn's right hand in requital, and bear away head and right hand to Tara, where they give them burial.

* * * * *

"There was a compact between the two Ulster champions to avenge each other. 'If I be the first killed,' said Cuchulainn, 'how soon wilt thou avenge me?' 'On thy death day before its evening.' And on his part Cuchulainn swore vengeance before Conall's blood was cold upon the earth.

"Conall pursues Lugaid and comes up with him. 'I am thy creditor for the slaying of my comrade, and here I stand suing thee for the debt.' At Lugaid's request Conall binds one hand to his side that they may fight on equal terms, but in the end overcomes him. 'Take my head,' says the dying warrior, 'and add my realm to thy realm, and my valour to thy valour. I prefer that thou shouldest be the best hero in Erin'."[86]

---

86 One may note here W. B. Yeats's *The Death of Cuchulain,* though it seems a none-too-lucid and in spots somewhat "arty" invention, and D. A. Mackenzie's minor "Cuchullén's Death," the latter in the *Celtic Review* (V, 128 ff.).

Of other miscellaneous tales concerning Cuchulainn, such as *The Tragical Death of Conlaech*,[87] a Sohrab-Rustum affair (a brief ninth-century relic in the *Yellow Book of Lecan*) in which the hero slays his own supposedly unrecognized son and is spelled to war the ocean waves to protect his fellows from his fury,[88] I choose for particularization here only *The Wooing of Emer, The Sickbed of Cuchulainn*, and *Bricriu's Feast*.

The Wooing of Emer[89] (of which two major redactions exist: Rawlinson MS. B.512 and the fuller Stowe MS. 992) has as its main theme the story of how messengers seek vainly throughout Ireland for a fitting wife for Cuchulainn, feeling—with reason—troubled about their own wives and daughters, and desiring him to beget an heir, since he is doomed to die young (and he *is* killed at the age of twenty-seven); and of how, consequently, Cuchulainn himself sets out to woo Emer, daughter of a wealthy landowner of Lusk named Forgall the Wily, she being reputedly the only girl in Ireland at the time having all of the famous six desirable womanly gifts. As shortly appears, the two converse in the secret language of the poets, Cuchulainn doing not a little boasting and Emer mocking him in banter. Her elder sister being unmarried, she tells him she cannot marry, but Cuchulainn will not have the elder because she once slept with Cairbre Niafer, son of the King of Ireland; eventually Emer agrees to

---

87 Ed. and trans. K. Meyer, *Ériu*, I, 114.—Cf. J. de Vries, "Le combat du père et du fils . . . ," *Ogam*, IX (1957), 122; Saul, *Carved in Findruine*.
88 Cf. W. B. Yeats's *Cuchulain's Fight with the Sea, On Baile's Strand*, and *The Only Jealousy of Emer* (in a prose reworking, *Fighting the Waves*). Yeats violates MS. tradition. For a curious variant out of oral tradition, see J. Curtin's "Cucúlin" in *Myths and Folk-Lore of Ireland* (Boston, 1890; copy. 1889), where the hero is one of Finn Mac Cumhall's "champions"!
89 See K. Meyer trans., Stowe MS., *Archæological Review*, I (1888).

marry him if he will slay a certain number of her relatives!

Forgall in disguise later visits Concobar's court and suggests that Cuchulainn go to Alba, to the Amazon Scathach ("Shadow"), in Skye, to perfect himself in arms. Cuchulainn follows his advice, first getting his promise of Emer on completion of the enterprise and also meeting Emer to exchange promises of chastity.

Many dangers and adventures befall Cuchulainn en route to Scathach's isle; but he arrives, promptly sleeps with Scathach's daughter (Uathach: "Apparition"—who has immediately fallen in love with him), perfects himself in arms, and later conquers Aife (? "Reflection": suggestion of Rees brothers—in any event, another Amazon, Scathach's enemy),[90] on whom he begets Conlaech. Other adventures follow during his return to Ireland and the year of fighting before he slays the guard and carries off Emer. When Concobar's *jus primae noctis* is pointed out by the nasty Bricriu, the nobles calm Cuchulainn by seeing that the privilege is only symbolically exercised—and one may add that, except for one major episode, the couple apparently live "happily ever after." That episode is recounted in the curious *Sickbed of Cuchulainn*,[91] wherein Fand, wife of Manannan Mac Lir, and her sister visit Ulster in the shape of birds—which Cuchulainn attempts, but fails, to kill. At night the two women visit him and,

---

[90] Variously in reference by Yeats, on whose miscellaneous use of Irish mythology one may consult the present author's *Prolegomena to the Study of Yeats's Poems* (Univ. of Pennsylvania Press, 1957) and *Prolegomena to the Study of Yeats's Plays* (Do., 1958).

[91] The earlier of two MSS. is in *The Book of the Dun Cow*. See O'Curry, *Manners and Customs . . .*, Lect. 9; and *The Sick-Bed of Cuchulainn* and *The Only Jealousy of Eimer* (Dublin, 1858). O'Curry first ed. and trans. the story in *Atlantis*, I and II.—W. S. Blunt's *Fand* was produced in part at the Abbey, 27 Apr. 1907.

smiling, beat the life almost out of him with horse switches. He is laid up speechless for a year. A messenger offers healing on condition that he come to Fand's country: Cuchulainn twice sends Laeg, his charioteer, instead, but finally himself goes to this beautiful land of immortals and spends a month with Fand, arranging a later tryst in Ulster. Discovering this, Emer, in her one real fit of jealousy, arms fifty maidens with knives and surprises the two—though presently she and Fand are with a rare courtesy both offering to give up the hero! Emer retains him in the end; then the much-absent husband Manannan appears to Fand, who says she will return, though she prefers Cuchulainn! Manannan then shakes his magic cloak, erasing all memory of the affair and preventing further meetings.

Bricriu's Feast,[92] verbose and composite in character, but a fairly good eighth-century story, recounts the evil-tongued poet's attempts to stir up trouble among the heroes by practically forcing attendance at the feast he provides and then manipulating the question of who (Conall, Loegaire, or Cuchulainn) shall get the "champion's portion" (an ancient consideration: cp. Dillon, *Irish Sagas*, 9-10), as well as that of which of the heroes' wives shall enjoy right of precedence. (There is almost grotesque humor in the picture of the three women, each accompanied by fifty retainers, hitching up their skirts to their hips and racing for the banqueting hall, which Cuchulainn subsequently raises on one side to admit Emer!) Matters are at long last resolved by the introduction of a beheading episode (suggestive of that later used in the

---

92 Earliest extant recording in *The Book of the Dun Cow*.

English romance *Sir Gawain and the Green Knight*), in which Cuchulainn's courage wins the hero both his challenger's desistance from the right to behead him in turn and permanent recognition of his own right to the champion's portion and his wife's right to precedence.—The beheading episode, incidentally, is recorded separately (*Gaelic MS., XL,* Edinburgh) as *The Bargain of the Strong Man,* or *The Champion's Covenant.*[93]

Among other Ulster tales especially worth recalling, *The Intoxication of the Ultonians*[94] is a grotesque fantasy telling of a nocturnal raid by the drunken heroes on the fort of Curoi Mac Dairi, in Kerry (a fort built to spin on its base at night for safety during Curoi's many absences)[95]: suffice it to say that the heroes just escape being roasted to death in an iron house; while *Mac Datho's Boar and Hound* is a brief, ancient tale of barbaric rivalry between Ulster and Connacht centering in a contest over carving Mac Datho's great boar: Conall Cearnach wins, boasting beforehand that he seldom sleeps without the head of a Connachtman as pillow![96]

---

[93] The last episode was edited and translated by K. Meyer in *Revue Celtique,* XIV, 450–59. For main text, with translation, see George Henderson's edn., Vol. II, Irish Texts Soc'y Pubns.—Cf. W. B. Yeats's *The Green Helmet*: in earlier prose version entitled *The Golden Helmet.* Yeats also introduces Cuchulainn into his weirdly moving *At the Hawk's Well,* as also elsewhere.

[94] *Mesca Ulad . . . ,* tr. W. M. Hennessey (Dublin, 1889). The *Book of Leinster* version lacks the end, the *Book of the Dun Cow,* the beginning, of this story.—On the Blandid story, cf. G. Keating, Comyn-Dinneen trans. of *Forus Feasa ar Éirinn, cit.,* II, 221–27.

[95] Cf. the ogre's house in Ella Young's *Unicorn with Silver Shoes.*—On revolving castles, see W. O. Sypherd, "Studies in Chaucer's *Hous of Fame,*" Chaucer Soc'y, Sec. Series, No. 39 (1907, for Issue of 1904).

[96] The oldest of several MS. versions of this popular story is that of the *Book of Leinster,* its theme perhaps of eighth-century rootage. There is a convenient summary in Best, "Old Irish Bardic Tales" (*United Irishman,* 6 Dec. 1902).—Cf. Saul, *Carved in Findruine.*

3. Fenian Cycle[97]

The Fenian—comprising ballads, prose tales, and tracts
—is the most popular of the great Irish cycles and contains by far the greatest number of individual stories; like
the others, it poses many problems as yet lacking scholarly
resolution—not to mention problems whose attempted
resolution has led to flat disagreement. For example, there
is the question of what the *Fianna* (or *Fena*), whose activities furnish the subject matter of the Cycle, really
were, though they have generally been conceived of as a
kind of extraordinary infantry (despite some mention of
horsemen) whose power and influence were most marked
during the reign of Cormac Mac Airt, when the king's
supposed son-in-law, Finn Mac Cumhall (most anciently
perhaps Find Mac Umall), was leader. It may be added
that Dillon, reasonably accepting Murphy's conclusion
seeing in Find "some kinship with" Lug(h), has claimed
that "The Fenian Cycle is not heroic saga at all, but
rather the remains of a lost mythology, of which the Celtic
god Lug was the central figure."[98] And despite Patrick
Joyce's opinion that the *Fianna* were an organization national in character, de Blacam says bluntly,[99] "Historically,
the Fianna never were a national army. Every State . . .
had its . . . *Fianna* . . ." (Meyer, writing more cautiously,
says that strictly "*fian* denoted a larger or smaller band of
roving warriors, who had joined for the purpose of mak-

---

[97] Cf. G. Henderson, "The Fionn Saga," *Celtic Review*, III; E. Mac Neill,
Duanaire Finn . . . (Vol. VII, Pubns. of the Irish Texts Soc'y: London,
1908; 2 more vols. ed. and trans. by G. Murphy: London, 1933, Dublin,
1953); A. Nutt, "Ossian and the Ossianic Literature," *Popular Studies*
. . . , No. 2 (London, 1899); G. Murphy, *The Ossianic Lore and Romantic Tales of Medieval Ireland* (Dublin, 1961).
[98] *Irish Sagas, cit.*, 13. Cf. Murphy, *cit.*, 8.
[99] *First Book of Irish Literature, cit.*, 65.

ing wars on their own account" and had legal recognition![100] And he adds[101] that the *Fianna*—named after their
leaders—"were held together by discipline, and had some
kind of organization and peculiar customs . . . ," remark-
ing further[102] that "The larger bands seem to have been
divided into companies of five or nine.")

According to Joyce, the peace-time strength of the
Fianna (the noun, incidentally, has etymologically no
connection with the name *Finn,* or *Fionn:* "fair-haired")
was nine thousand; the war-time, twenty-one thousand:
and there were strict enrollment tests—*e.g.,* every pro-
spective warrior had to have mastered a stipulated quan-
tity of literary matter in prose and verse. When not
training or fighting, the *Fianna* reportedly spent the six
warm months of the year hunting and camping, the six
cold months as guests of the well-to-do. Their constituent
clans are pictured as sometimes at odds with each other,
as were Finn's Clann Baiscinn, of Leinster, and Goll Mac
Morna's Clann Morna, of Connacht, because Goll had
slain Finn's father at the battle of Cnucha.

Being essentially infantry, the *Fianna* built few, if any,
forts and rejected chariots; but were great athletes. It is
reported that they sometimes fought against their own
monarch, eventually becoming so troublesome that Cairbre had to fight them to virtual annihilation at Gabhra
(Meath), though he himself was slain in the battle
(A.D. 297). Finn is their greatest figure, though not seldom presented in the sagas as a sometimes unpleasant
fellow; among other leaders are Oisin ("Usheen"—

---

[100] *Fianaigecht,* Todd Lecture Series, Royal Irish Academy, Vol. XVI
(Dublin & London, 1910), rpt. of 1937, p. ix.
[101] *Ibid.,* xi.
[102] *Ibid.,* fn. 1.

Scotch *Ossian*), Finn's poet-son by Saeve (a *ben-side*[103])
—and Oisin's "brave and gentle" son Oscar, Diarmuid
O'Duibhne (tragically constrained to become the lover of
Grainne), Cailte Mac Ronain, Conan Mail—"the Bald"
(a gross and cowardly braggart), and Goll Mac Morna.

Well, after Brian Boru's victory over the Norse at
Clontarf (1014) there is supposed to have developed a
national resurgence, with emergence into wide popularity
of the Fenian tales and ballads—a popularity destined to
persist for centuries. It appears possible that the earliest
Fenian stories were cast in the form of eighth-century
lays, though in general extant manuscripts seem seldom
to argue linguistically for composition prior to the
twelfth century, to which belongs the prose *Colloquy* . . . ,
presently to be noticed, which in a sense represents the
culmination of the cycle. Indeed, the majority of the
manuscripts appear datable from the twelfth to the nine-
teenth century.

Finn—who appears variously as patriot, rebel, dragon-
slayer, and general hero—has been claimed by both
Munster and Leinster, though the latter's claim seems the
more authentic. Eleanor Hull, in a theory admittedly not
entirely her own, accounts him really a member of the
subjugated Firbolg race, among whose members she
thinks the Fenian tales actually originated.[104] This view
explains for her the "slow acceptance of the tales," since
"the great bulk of the written Ossianic Literature comes
to us from the late fifteenth century onward," even though
she counts it possible that the Fenian legend "is in its

---

[103] Cf. Stephens, "Oisin's Mother," *Irish Fairy Tales*.
[104] See "Origin of the Fenian Tales," *Text-Book* . . . , *cit.*, II, Ch. III. Cf.
James Stephens' intro. to Figgis, *Return of the Hero*, and Mac Neill,
cit. next fn.

origin older than the Cuchulain cycle." Noticing the essentially *folk* interests and qualities in the Fenian tales (*e.g.,* the popularity of hunting, the frank delight in fairy lore, the democratic tone, etc.), she fancies the Gaelic ruling classes preferred the aristocratic tales of the Ulster Cycle, whereas the Fenian tales were the delight of the folk and had to win their way to general acceptance despite the neglect of the early poets. Of course, in this case general acceptance brought with it amazing popularity, in Scotland as well as in Ireland (one recalls the absurdly sentimental forgeries of the Scot Macpherson in this connection), and an uncounted number of lays and stories, authentically the property of the people. Thus, in Miss Hull's view, the whole history of the Fenian Cycle represents a triumph of "the imagination of a subjected race, regarded as outcast by their conquerors, but whose traditions, as the race distinction slowly died out, became the heritage of the entire nation." On the other hand, it is Hyde's opinion that, as compared with the Red Branch tales, most of the Fenian pieces "are more modern in conception and surroundings. There is little or no mention of the war chariot. . . . The Fenians fought on foot or horseback, and we meet, too, frequent mention of helmets and mailcoats, which are post-Danish touches. Things are on a smaller scale."[105]

---

[105] *Literary History . . . , cit.,* 374. Mac Neill, however, whose views jump with Miss Hull's, insists vigorously (*Duanaire Finn,* xliii): ". . . the story of Fionn appears to have arisen, like most primitive hero-lore, in the region of mythology. It obtained a peculiar development among the ancient vassal race of North Leinster, the Galeoin, who impressed on the life of the heroes the character of professional warriorship, permanent military service being a special obligation of unfree races only. Ignored by the dominant peoples, the story in this form spread widely among the subject states, and received various local developments. By the ninth century, it had begun to be written down. The old ideas of racial inequality had then lost most of their force; the status of permanent military service had long ceased to be prevalent; and so the

Of the huge number of stories belonging to the Fenian Cycle,[106] only a few of the most vital and representative need be here recalled. Of these, *The Cause of the Battle of Cnucha* and *The Boy-Deeds of Finn* will serve to introduce the cyclic sequence.

The brief *Cause of the Battle of Cnucha* (modern Castleknock, near Dublin), composed not later than the eleventh century (perhaps much earlier), recorded in the *Book of the Dun Cow,* and supposedly concerned with events of the late second century, tells how Cumhall, son of Trenmor, a warrior in Conn's service, having been refused Muirne, daughter of the druid Tadg, son of Nuada, carried her off by force—and had, in consequence, to fight the allied forces of Conn, Aedh ("Fire") Mac Morna, and Urgrend at Cnucha. Cumhall was slain by Aedh, but the latter lost an eye in the battle and was thereafter called Goll ("One-eyed"). Threatened with burning by her father, the pregnant Muirne was sent by Conn to Cumhall's married sister for her confinement, and bore Deimne, later called Finn. When the boy reached fighting age, he forced Tadg to pay *eric* (in the form of

---

stories of the Fiana came gradually to be accepted even by the dominant race on their merits as literature. Unfettered by prestige, the sagas were susceptible of unlimited development, and were free to adapt themselves to popular taste. In time they ousted all their rivals."—O'Rahilly, by the way, asserts (*Early Irish History and Mythology, cit.,* 277) anent "Finn and his *fian*": " . . . none of their alleged achievements has the remotest connection with history. Finn and his fellows . . . never existed." Murphy, as indicated earlier (see fn. 98), also feels that Finn was "originally a mythological figure."

106 In general connection with which the vivid post-Victorian rehandlings by James Stephens in *Irish Fairy Tales* and Ella Young in *The Tangle-Coated Horse* deserve most emphatic particularization as remarkably beautiful works. For an interesting post-Cyclic Fenian tale, see "How Fin Went to the Kingdom of the Big Men," in *More Celtic Fairy Tales,* ed. J. Jacobs (London, 1894), or J. G. Campbell's *The Fiana* (London, 1891). One may also name here, in miscellaneous modern reference, Flann O'Brien's *At Swim-Two-Birds* and James Joyce's ubiquitous *Finnegans Wake.*

the territory of Almu, Leinster) for his father's death and
concluded a sort of uneasy peace with Goll, whose Clann
Morna also paid *eric*.

The Boy-Deeds of Finn[107] is an unfinished twelfth-
century tale, nourished by a tradition varying from that in
which the story just outlined is rooted, and recorded in
MS. Laud 610 (fifteenth century). After a brief account
of the battle of Cnucha, it rehearses Finn's rearing in the
forest (for safety's sake, since Morna's people were seeking his death) by Bodball (Cumhall's sister) and "the
Grey One of Luachar," Liath Luachra, two women warriors. Thereafter are recounted, among other things, his
winning a youthful hurley contest (as did the child Cuchulainn), his getting named "Finn" because of his fair-
ness, and his exploits as hunter and fighter prior to his
going to study poetry with Finn-eigeas and chancing to
taste the "Salmon of Knowledge" (through burning his
thumb while cooking the fish for his mentor)—after
which he had merely to suck his thumb when he desired
knowledge or guidance.

After Finn has achieved leadership of the *Fianna*
(though the underlying hatred of Goll and his relatives
is a constant danger, as such tales as *The Brawl at Alm-
hain*—Allen, Co. Kildare—indicate), numerous adventures and undertakings of a highly romantic—sometimes
grotesque—character ensue. These are recorded in ballads
and stories like *The Cave of Ceiscorann,* * The Birth of
Bran,* * The Carle of the Drab Coat,* * The Battle of Cnoc
an Air,* * The Festivities at the House of Conan of Ceann*

---

107 Cf. version by J. O'Donovan, *Transactions of Ossianic Soc'y*, IV.—
For variant oral tradition, cf. "Birth of Fin Mac Cumhail" in J. Curtin's
Myths and Folk-Lore of Ireland, cit. This collection includes nine tales
assimilated to Fenian tradition.—Cf. K. Meyer, "Boyish Exploits of
Finn," *Ériu*, I, 180 ff.

Sleibhe,* The Adventures of the Lomnochtan of Slieve Riffé, The Kern of the Narrow Stripes, The Battle of the White Strand,* The Hunt at Slieve Cuillin,* The House of the Quicken Trees, and *The Pursuit of the Giolla Decair**—to list a handful of the most popular, starred titles being those of versions conveniently available in Lady Gregory's *Gods and Fighting Men* (London and New York, 1904). Summaries of the last three named will suggest the characteristic nature of the best of these.

The Hunt at Slieve Cuillin[108] (one of the stories told St. Patrick by Oisin) recalls how the Dé Danann smith Culand's two daughters, Milucra and Aina, both loved Finn. The latter having once remarked she would never marry a grey-haired man, Milucra has the Dé Danann folk make her a lake on Slieve Cuillin, whose waters she enchants in order that they may gray the hair of any mortal bather. Lured by a doe, later, Finn and his two hounds give chase all the way from Almu to this lake, where Finn finds a woman bewailing the loss of a gold ring in the waters. Placed under *geasa,* he seeks and finds it for her—whereupon she jumps into the lake and disappears. Stepping out, Finn finds himself old and decrepit, unrecognized by his own dogs. Oisin and Cailte presently lead a search for him. Successful, they learn how Culand's daughter has bewitched him; so the *Fianna* later dig their way into her *síd,* where Finn is given a restorative drink, though by choice he retains his gray hair.

In *The House of the Quicken* [Mountain Ash] *Trees,*[109] Colga, King of Lochlann, invades Ireland in

---

108 Numerous Royal Irish Academy MSS.; trans. by Joyce in *Old Celtic Romances.*
109 Royal Irish Academy MSS. 23.C.30., 24.B.15., 23.L.24.; trans. by Joyce, *Old Celtic Romances.*—For variants of the essential story out of oral tradition, see "Fin Mac Cumhail and the Fenians of Erin in the

Cormac Mac Airt's day; Cormac sends word to Finn, and the *Fianna* muster. After a hard battle, the *Fianna* emerge victorious, Colga having been slain by Oscar. Colga's son Midac (the only one of the Lochlann nobility to be spared) is taken into Finn's household to be reared and given a place among the *Fianna*. But the boy grows up meditating revenge, and on Conan's advice is eventually separated from Finn's household, but generously given two cantreds of his choice. Here he lives isolated from his former associates for fourteen years, after which he reappears to put Finn and a group of companions under *geasa* to attend a feast in his House of the Quicken Trees.

Finn and a group of his chiefs go, Oisin and certain others keeping watch near by. The splendid palace they enter seems empty; presently Midac looks in, but leaves, silent—whereupon they find the place transformed into a smoky room with one door and it locked, and themselves held fixed to the earthen floor by enchantment. Then Finn's "tooth of knowledge" informs them that Midac has assembled outside forces to slay them—and even floored the room where they are helpless with enchanted clay supplied by the three kings of the "Island of the Torrent" (whose sprinkled blood alone can break the enchantment). So the group sound, though rather sadly, their *dord fiansa,* or "war-cry."

By twilight, Oisin, lacking a promised messenger from Finn, gets worried. Finn's son Ficna and his foster son Innsa go to the enchanted house and learn the truth. The latter undertakes to defend the ford by which the house must be approached, while the former reconnoiters. After

Castle of Fear Dubh" and "Fin Mac Cumhail and the Son of the King of Alba," in Curtin's *Myths and Folk-Lore of Ireland, cit.*

a heroic defense, Innsa is slain; then Ficna avenges his death, replaces him, and repels a second attack.

Next Midac leads a picked band against the ford, and Diarmuid and a companion go to aid Ficna. Diarmuid sends his spear through Midac, who nevertheless slays the over-worn Ficna. Diarmuid then beheads Midac as *eric* for Finn; then he accedes to the request of the glutton Conan (one of Finn's immediate companions) and fetches food and drink to him from the drunken revelers of Midac's gathering, though he has to pour the wine through a hole in the roof into Conan's large mouth.

Diarmuid and his companion Fatha then guard the ford—and eventually Diarmuid slays the three kings of the "Island of the Torrent" and releases Finn and his group by sprinkling the enchanted clay with their blood, though the released Fenians must await sunrise for returning strength. So Diarmuid and Fatha must withstand alone till sunrise an attack by Borba, son of Sinsar, King of the World.[110] Finally day comes and Finn and his men join the battle, Goll slaying Borba. Meanwhile word has been sent to Oisin.

Then Sinsar gathers his hosts and advances; at the same time Oisin appears with the *Fianna* and a furious battle is joined. Finally Oscar makes for King Sinsar and, after a terrible struggle, beheads him. The remnants of the routed enemy then flee to their ships.

The Pursuit of the Giolla Decair ("Bad Servant"),[111] one of the most marvelous and beautiful of the Fenian

---

110 *Borb*: "proud."—Arthur is called "King of the World" in *The Story of a Crop-Eared Dog* (Vol. X, Irish Texts Soc'y Pubns.: London, 1908—for 1907).
111 Royal Irish Academy MSS. 24.B.28. and 23.G.21.; trans. by Joyce, *Old Celtic Romances*. Cf. Young, *cit.,* fn. 106.

tales, recounts how Finn, after giving a sort of national feast, begins with his *Fianna* a summer chase through Munster. At his request for a volunteer, Finn Ban Mac Bresal goes to watch from the peak of Collkilla to spot any possible Dé Danann mischief. Shortly he sees an armed and repulsive Fomorian giant approaching him from the east and leading a revolting horse. Frightened, he goes to Finn and his comrades, whom the monster approaches respectfully, requesting a year's service under Finn with the privilege of naming his own wage at the end, but stating that he eats at each meal as much as a hundred ordinary men and that he is called the *Giolla Decair* because of his laziness and general human incompatibility. Finn, in accordance with a custom of his, accedes. Finding the cavalry are twice as well paid as the infantry, the *Giolla* assigns himself to the former and, having placed the brute under the protection of Finn and the *Fianna* about him, turns his horse loose among those of the miscellaneous *Fianna*. The brute viciously damages them all and then starts for Conan Mail's personal horses. Angered, Conan is forced to put a halter on the animal's neck—whereupon the horse stands still, remaining immovable though fourteen others, beating and kicking, join Conan on his back. Seeing this, the *Giolla Decair* pretends anger, leaves Finn's service, and heads southwest, the horse promptly following—with the fifteen *Fianna* unable to get off. Finn and the rest pursue, but the horse heads into the sea, Ligan Lumina ("The bounding Ligan," who has managed to grasp his tail) dragged along as a helpless sixteenth while the waters open to a dry road before them, closing in behind as they progress.

En route, on the poet Fergus Finnvel's advice, to get a certain ship, Finn and his fellows meet two brothers who request service, the one gifted at magical ship-building, the other at tracking both by sea and by land! So Finn engages them—and has ship and pilot at once to trail the *Giolla Decair*. Then he chooses fifteen men and departs, leaving Oisin behind to command the remaining *Fianna*. Sailing westward, they pass through storm to approach a glassy cliff rising from the waters, where the *Giolla Decair's* track seems to end. Then Diarmuid O'Duibhne, taunted by the poet Fergus, scales the cliff and finds a beautiful plain stretching inland. Having drunken from a well at hand, he is approached by a *gruagach,* whom he fights till dusk, when the giant leaps into the well and disappears. Then Diarmuid spears a deer for his supper and later sleeps by his fire till sunrise, when he slays another deer for breakfast, drinking as usual from the well. The giant reappears for another day-long fight and evening disappearance.

At the end of the fourth day of fighting, Diarmuid clasps his opponent and is carried down the well with him to *Tir-fa-tonn* ("Country-under-wave"), where the giant wrenches himself free and escapes to a palace, in front of which Diarmuid puts to flight a great company of opponents, thereafter—most confidently!—going to sleep on the battleground. He is awakened by a friendly young prince who takes him home, has him bathed and healed of wounds, and refreshes him. Later the prince reveals himself as the deprived brother of the king (the "Knight of the Fountain" who had fought Diarmuid), on whom he plans war with Diarmuid's aid, which is pledged.

Meanwhile Finn and the rest succeed in scaling the cliff—and are welcomed by the King of Sorca and his nobles, whom they presently aid in driving off the attacking King of the World. Then Diarmuid approaches with a company, having slain the King of *Tir-fa-tonn* and made his host, the "Knight of Valor," ruler; he tells how the latter has druidically revealed that it was really Avarta, a Dé Danann, in the shape of the *Giolla Decair*, who carried the sixteen *Fianna* away to *Tir Tairrngire* ("Land of Promise"). So Finn and his party resume voyaging till they find the "Land of Promise," where Manannan Mac Lir had reared Diarmuid, and send heralds to Avarta, who, after consultation, decides not to risk war with the *Fianna*. So Finn and his comrades are royally entertained and offered *eric*. Finn declines, but Conan demands that fifteen of Avarta's noblest friends mount the famous horse and, with Avarta himself clinging to the tail, go back to Ireland by the same route the *Fianna* were carried away on. The *Fianna* return home and Avarta (again in the shape of the *Giolla Decair*) fulfills Conan's demand—after which he disappears with his fellows from the midst of the *Fianna*.

Of other Fenian tales, an *aithed* (elopement story), *The Pursuit of Diarmuid and Grainne*,[112] has achieved what many, considering both structure and content, may count an ill-deserved fame. Apparently unreferred to before the tenth century, and with a manuscript tradition no older than the fourteenth or fifteenth, it tells how Finn, at the time an old widower who has decided to rewed, is advised to seek Grainne, daughter of Cormac Mac Airt. Despite long enmity between Finn and Cormac, amicable arrangements are concluded; but at the betrothal banquet Grainne decides she prefers a younger man—and conse-

---

[112] Text and trans. by S. H. O'Grady, *Transactions of the Ossianic Soc'y,* 1855; oldest extant text (1651), Royal Irish Academy MS. 24.P.9.—Joyce has a trans. in *Old Celtic Romances.*—Cf. Gertrude Schoepperle, *Tristan and Isolt* (2 v.; Frankfurt a. M. & London, 1913). See also J. Carney, *Studies in Irish Literature and History* (Dublin, 1955).

quently drugs all the banqueters but Oisin and Diarmuid, to whom, respectively, she offers herself. Both refuse; so she puts Diarmuid under *geasa* to elope with her the same night. He necessarily accedes, going with her, then and thenceforth, unwillingly. The rest of the verbose story details Finn's pursuit, with his own *Fianna* constantly trying to protect the couple from him, Diarmuid being the very model of a beloved and outstanding fellow-warrior. In the end, Finn accomplishes Diarmuid's death in treacherous and ignoble fashion after the hero has been wounded by the ferocious boar into which his foster brother had been metamorphosed (O'Grady recalls Adonis)—whereupon, according to one of varying manuscript traditions, Grainne marries him (to the disgust of the *Fianna*), even managing to reconcile Diarmuid's sons (whom she had sent to be trained for vengeance by Bolcan, "the smith of hell") to service under Finn.[113]

After the tragic annihilation of the *Fianna* at Gabhra (Garristown, Co. Dublin: see poem in *Transactions, Ossianic Society,* I), following Cairbre's attempted dissolution of Clann Baiscinn and the clan's entering the service of the King of Munster (all this leading to the final battle between it and Clann Morna), the thread of story leads to the accounts of Oisin in *Tír-na-nÓg* ("Land of the Young") and the various dialogues between that old hero and St. Patrick.

Oisin in the Land of the Young,[114] one of the stories in question, is clearly of modern shaping, though in part its

---

[113] This popular, but curiously unpleasant, story has been variously retold in English; *e.g.,* Yeats and Moore once collaborated on a lame dramatic version, and Lady Gregory, in *Grania,* achieved some novelty of interpretation. Austin Clarke's *The Vengeance of Fionn* is an effective reworking; Katharine Tynan has a piece in *Shamrocks* (London, 1887). See Joyce, *Old Celtic Romances,* for one version.

[114] Again, Joyce has a translation in *Old Celtic Romances.*

incidents recall the ancient *Adventures of Connla* and *Cormac's Adventures. . . .*[115] One version was written, in dialogue form and in verse imitative of bardic conventions, by the eighteenth-century Michael Comyn. Herein, replying to kindly questions asked by St. Patrick, the blind and aged Oisin tells how, while he was hunting with Finn and a group of other survivors of Gabhra, the incredibly beautiful Niam ("Beauty") came to woo him away to *Tír-na-nÓg* on a magic steed; how he enjoyed with her that land of youth-forever-renewed for three hundred

---

[115] These belong to the "king stories." In *The Adventures of Connla* (a brief and charming tale, probably of eighth-century origin: oldest recension in the *Book of the Dun Cow;* text and trans. by J. O'B. Crowe, *Kilkenny Archæological Journal,* 1874–75 vol.), the hero, son of Conn of the Hundred Battles and brother to Art, sees while standing on the Hill of Usnech with his father and the druid Corann a beautiful girl come to woo him to Mag Mell ("The Pleasant Plain"), promising a life of youth and beauty until Judgment Day in this *sid* of King Boadach the Eternal. The others can hear and speak with, but not see, this fairy girl. Conn appeals to his druid and Corann drives her away—but not before she tosses Connla an apple, which—eaten of but never diminished—becomes his whole sustenance for a month, when the girl returns. Hearing her again, Conn calls for his druid; she reproaches him, prophesying St. Patrick's coming. Questioned, Connla admits his longing, and, on further appeal, leaps into the girl's crystal boat, in which the two depart forever. Conn looks on Art and says, "Today is Art left the lone one": hence, *Art Oenfer* ("Art the Lonely").

In *Cormac's Adventures in the Land of Promise (Book of Fermoy),* Cormac, son of Art, grants an unknown warrior, in exchange for a magical bell-branch, three requests—and thus loses his daughter Ailbe, his son Cairbre, and his wife Ethne Taebfada. Following the third forfeit, Cormac, leading a pursuit of the warrior, is isolated in a mist, though eventually he comes on two marvelous strongholds, in one of which he is entertained and has his family restored to him unharmed. It appears that the unknown warrior was Manannan, King of the Land of Promise, who wanted to draw Cormac on a visit. In the end, Cormac and his family are magically returned to Tara, with the bell-branch and a magic cup to be the king's possession for life. The whole relatively pointless story seems quasi-allegorical and moralistic in purport. R. K. Alspach ("Some Sources of Yeats's *The Wanderings of Oisin,*" *PMLA,* LVIII, 3. 863–65) remarks on Yeats's use of the bell-branch in the *Oisin* and *The Dedication to a Book of Stories Selected from the Irish Novelists.*—See W. Stokes, *Irische Texte,* iii,1; S. H. O'Grady, *Transactions, Ossianic Soc'y,* III. Cf. "How Cormac Mac Art Went to Faery," *More Celtic Fairy Tales,* ed. J. Jacobs, *cit.*

years, fathering two sons and a daughter by her; how homesickness called him to revisit Ireland, though Niam warned him Finn and all his former comrades were dead; how he returned on the understanding that if he touched foot to his native soil he would never be able to return to *Tir-na-nÓg;* and how, appealed to, he lifted and flung a great slab of marble to aid some struggling laborers— with the result that he broke the magic steed's saddle girth and accidentally touched earth, to become the pitiful creature of Patrick's acquaintance.[116]

The Colloquy of the Ancients,[117] finally, the leading and longest prose piece of the Cycle, written about 1200—or earlier, its oldest (fifteenth-century) recensions in the *Book of Lismore* and MS Laud 610, is really a set of "frame" stories in which Cailte, Oisin, and eighteen comrades are pictured as having survived Gabhra by one hundred and fifty years. Oisin goes to visit his mother Blaí in the *sid* of Ucht Cleitig; Cailte and his group chance on Patrick and his clerics at Drumderg—and a charming courtesy prevails all around, Patrick having dispersed with holy water the devils looming attendant above the ancients! His guardian angels order Patrick to record the old warriors' stories; so the Fenians are baptized and the band traipse about Ireland en route to Tara, different spots recalling different tales, thus evoking a sort of *dinn-*

---

116 The story is most beautifully retold in Yeats's *The Wanderings of Oisin,* though herein Patrick is not exactly a lovable or sympathetic figure; there is a spottily memorable prose version in Darrell Figgis' *The Return of the Hero.*—Comyn's version (*c.* 1750) may be read in a translation by Thomas Flannery (Dublin, 1896). A curious and amusing variant is "Oisin in Tir na n-Og," in Curtin's *Myths and Folk-Lore of Ireland, cit.*—One may also cf. James Stephens, "Oisin and Niamh," *Sinn Féin,* 26 Feb. 1910; and George Brandon Saul, "The Trial by Fable," *Poet Lore,* VI, rev. version in *Hound and Unicorn.*
117 Edns. by O'Grady (*Silva Gadelica,* 1892—trans. in Vol. II), Stokes (1900), Nessa Ní Shéaghda (3 v.; 1942–45).

shenchus ("place-history"). These stories, some two hundred, uneven in length and kind, as is to be expected, are an amazing mixture, with songs interspersed. Unfortunately, the end of the *Colloquy* is lacking.

It may be added, in concluding this reminder of wizard beauty long burning under time, that according to some apparently late stories, Finn was after his passing reincarnated as Mongán, begotten by Manannan Mac Lir on the wife of Fiachna, King of Ulster![118]

* * * * * * *

This in memory of the Brandons before me.

---

[118] Cf., again, Stephens, *Irish Fairy Tales.*—According to one of the Mongán stories, this begetting was Manannan's price for saving the life of Fiachna while that king was away aiding Aedan of Scotland against the Saxons (cf. *The Voyage of Bran*); according to another, the revelation that Mongán is really Finn is made by Cailte (returned from the dead) in settling a disagreement between Mongán and the poet Forgall over the question of where Fothad Airgdech was slain—and thus averting the threatened loss by Mongán of his wife, demanded by Forgall as a satisfaction in lieu of satirization of the king.

INDEX OF NAMES

111